BARASSI

TEE O'NEILL

CURRENCY PRESS

CURRENCY PLAYS

First published in 2012
by Currency Press Pty Ltd,
PO Box 2287, Strawberry Hills, NSW, 2012, Australia
enquiries@currency.com.au
www.currency.com.au

in association with Jager Productions

Copyright: © Tee O'Neill, 2012.

NATIONAL LIBRARY OF AUSTRALIA CIP DATA

Author:	O'Neill, Tee.
Title:	Barassi / Tee O'Neill.
ISBN:	9780868199597 (pbk.)
Subjects:	Barassi, Ron, 1936—Drama.
	Australian football players—Drama
	Australian football coaches—Drama.
Dewey Number:	A822.3

Typeset by Dean Nottle for Currency Press.
Printed by Hyde Park Press, Richmond, SA.
Cover image by 3 Deep Design.
Cover design by Alan Jager.

Contents

Theatre Program at the end of the playtext

Barassi was commissioned and originally produced by Jager Productions in Melbourne, Victoria. It premiered at the Athenaeum Theatre, Melbourne on 26 September 2012 with the following cast:

BARASSI	Steve Bastoni
BARASSI JR & SENIOR	Chris Asimos
NORM SMITH	Matt Parkinson
MELBA	Jane Clifton
ELZA/NANCY/CHERRYL/	
HOPKINS /ENSEMBLE	Amanda LaBonte
MUELLER/KYNE/MANTELLO/	
ENSEMBLE	Richard Sutherland
ENSEMBLE/SYD JACKSON	Glenn Maynard
ENSEMBLE/BRENT CROSSWELL	Russell Robertson
ENSEMBLE/ALEX JESAULENKO	Bartholomew Walsh

Other parts played by members of the company.

Director, Terence O'Connell
Set Designer, Nathan Weyers
AV Designer, Kim O'Connell
Lighting Designer, Jason Bovaird
Sound Designer, Paul Norton
Costume Designer, Kim Bishop
Choreographer, Alana Scanlan
Producer, Alan Jager in association with Hit Productions

CHARACTERS

PHIL MANASSA, Collingwood footballer

MELBA, 62, omniscient narrator

BARASSI, 29–45 years old (and briefly 72), Super Coach of Carlton, North Melbourne, Melbourne and Sydney Swans

BARASSI JR, from physically awkward 14-year-old to champion player and captain of Melbourne Football Club in his 20s

SENIOR, Ron Barassi's father

NORM SMITH, champion player and coach of Melbourne

ELZA, 26–early 50s, Barassi's mother

JACK MUELLER, Melbourne Football Club's seconds coach

COLIN BREWSTER, Barassi's stepfather

NANCY, 20–35, Barassi's first wife

PHONSE KYNE, legendary coach of Collingwood

MURRAY WEIDEMAN, Collingwood footballer

BARRY 'HOOKER' HARRISON, Collingwood footballer

NEIL 'FROGGY' CROMPTON, Melbourne footballer

INTERVIEWER, journalist in 1965

GEORGE HARRIS, president of Carlton Football Club

BUTCHER 1

BUTCHER 2

ALEX JESAULENKO, Carlton footballer

BRENT CROSSWELL, Carlton footballer

SYD JACKSON, Aboriginal Carlton footballer

TEDDY HOPKINS, 19, Carlton footballer

ALBERT MANTELLO, vice-president of North Melbourne

DES TUDDENHAM, captain-coach of Essendon

CHERRYL, 30s–40s, Barassi's second wife

MARK 'WHACKO' JACKSON, flamboyant Melbourne footballer

SERGEANT, ghost in Tobruk

PRIVATE, ghost in Tobruk

WARWICK CAPPER, Sydney Swans footballer

CASTING

Nine actors (seven male, two female) play all roles. The actors play the major roles in the following groupings.

Male 1:

BARASSI: Deeply focused, short-fused man who shows everything he is thinking and feeling on his expressive face. A great motivator, he has no patience for people who aren't hard-working and willing to give their utmost to the game.

Male 2:

BARASSI JR

BARASSI SENIOR, An amiable rover who loves a laugh and is a very determined football player.

Male 3:

NORM: Dignified, highly principled coach of the Melbourne Football Club. Although we see him in one scene as a 25-year-old, he is mainly in his 40s but looking older.

Male 4:

MUELLER: Grumpy and hates players getting too big for their boots.

KYNE: Passionate legendary Collingwood coach.

MANTELLO: Lives for the North Melbourne Football Club.

ENSEMBLE MEMBER 5

Male 5:

JESAULENKO: From Canberra, Ukrainian heritage amiable champion footballer.

COLIN: Earnest but affable stepfather of Barassi.

ENSEMBLE MEMBER 3

Male 6:

JACKSON: Playful champion Aboriginal player.

ENSEMBLE MEMBER 1

Male 7:

CROSSWELL: Champion footballer and intellectual.

MANASSA: Kicked the 'Goal of the Century' in 1977.

ENSEMBLE MEMBER 2

Female 1:

MELBA: Very lively, omniscient narrator. She is wise, ironic and shapes the events of the show.

Female 2:

ELZA: Warm, loving, but unsentimental.

NANCY: Loyal, bright and shy.

CHERRYL: Bohemian and opinionated.

HOPKINS: Blonde-mopped Hopkins surprises everyone, except Barassi, when he kicks four glorious goals in the second half of the 1970 Grand Final.

ENSEMBLE MEMBER 4

The six ENSEMBLE MEMBERS make up a chorus of FOOTBALLERS from Melbourne, Carlton and North Melbourne, COMMENTATORS, SUPPORTERS, JOURNALISTS and OTHER ROLES.

NOTES ON PUNCTUATION

— means an interruption

… means the thought has trailed off

/ indicates the beginning of an overlap in dialogue

Words inside brackets [like these] are thought but not said.

This play went to press before the end of rehearsals and may differ from the play as performed.

ACT ONE

As the house lights dim MELBA *and three* ENSEMBLE MEMBERS *are gossiping in the wings of the theatre. The following dialogue is heard but unseen.*

ENSEMBLE 2: Thought it happened on Lygon Street.

MELBA: No, Fitzroy Street.

ENSEMBLE 3: My cousin's boss knew the woman that got hit.

ENSEMBLE 1: Right, so he's sitting at a restaurant and sees a woman: getting hit.

ENSEMBLE 2: Fly-tackles the guy.

MELBA: Like he was chasin' a Sherrin.

ENSEMBLE 3: What was he thinking?

ENSEMBLE 2: Thought he was on the MCG.

MELBA: Instinctive. See damsel in distress and bang!

ENSEMBLE 2: Straight to it.

ENSEMBLE 3: Playin' the man.

MELBA: Like '58.

ENSEMBLE 1: He's an old bugger.

ENSEMBLE 2: Old fella takin' on 20-year-olds, heart as big as Phar Lap.

MELBA: It's instinctive, he sees a bloke bash a woman.

ENSEMBLE 2: He bolts at him.

ENSEMBLE 3: Like Superman.

ENSEMBLE 1: Pulls him to the ground.

MELBA: Into the gutter where the woman-beating weasel belongs.

ENSEMBLE 2: Chase-down tackle by Barass!

ENSEMBLE 1: But didn't he get kicked?

MELBA: They kicked him, yeah, kept kicking him.

ENSEMBLE 1: Who kicked him?

ENSEMBLE 3: The woman's basher.

MELBA: And his cowardly mates.

ENSEMBLE 1: Where's the headspace to kick an old bloke?

ENSEMBLE 3: Did they know who they were kicking?

ENSEMBLE 2: Did they realise the man they could have killed?

MELBA: I think the show has started.

ENSEMBLE: [*all*] Shit!

> *SLIDE: A huge slide reads:*
> '*BARASSI: THE STAGE SHOW*
> *THIS STORY IS TRUE*
> *MOST OF IT ACTUALLY HAPPENED* '
> *The lights snap to dark.*

SCENE ONE: MANASSA'S GOAL OF THE CENTURY

In the dark.

Noise of a crowd of 100,000 people.

Emerging in slow motion from the wings is a 1970s Collingwood football player—PHIL MANASSA. *He is wearing number 31. He has long hair and sideburns; fit but not athletic.*

MANASSA *has just got possession of the ball and he runs—breaking free and bolting away from his North Melbourne opponents.*

The crowd noise surges with excitement.

MANASSA *bounces, sees he's still free, then puts the ball under his arm, running huge strides, he bounces the ball again, he goes to handpass, retains the ball, dodging a player and as he steps out of view we know he is about to go for goal.*

The crowd noise surges. Collingwood supporters are wild with happiness.

Underneath the noise we struggle to hear the following football commentary gradually getting louder.

RADIO COMMENTATOR: Manassa out from halfback flank—goes for a run along towards the forward line, runs 50 metres, takes the handball, no, claims the handball, he shoots for goal and, [*clearly audible now*] he puts it through! He puts it through! By golly! That's got to be the goal of the century and making the Magpies still in line to win the 1977 Grand Final.

> *The triumphant* MANASSA *runs back on holding the back of his head in happiness and exits.*

> *A woman,* MELBA, *wearing a Melbourne Cricket Club tour guide uniform and a Collingwood football scarf, cranks a scoreboard to read:*

Collingwood 8.7.55, North Melbourne 9.12.66

The sound of the match continues as MELBA *speaks to the audience.*

MELBA: [*to the audience*] It's the 1977 Grand Final and Collingwood is facing the Barassi-coached North Melbourne. Barassi's Kangaroos may be ahead but the whiff of victory has entered the Magpies nostrils.

The crowd cries out as a goal is kicked.

Not since 1958 have we felt this—hope, hope. Feel the hope in the crowd. Hope for Collingwood. Hope for ourselves! When the siren sounded last week on 100,000 dreams, it was the second ever drawn Grand Final in VFL history. The city of Melbourne had to endure another 168 hours of unexpressed emotion. But for Magpie supporters it has been 168 hundred *thousand* hours waiting for Collingwood to win the Grand Final again. And now, right now, we are in a state of the sweetest anguish. Last week Barassi's Kangaroos were also in front but the Shinboners did not score a goal in the third and fourth quarters and the Mighty Pies caught up to them to equal the scoreboard. You just saw Collingwood's Phil Manassa kick the goal of the 20th century. The '77 flag could easily be ours!

Portions of the crowd are beginning to call out.

CROWD: Barassi! Barassi! Barassi!

MELBA: Ronald Dale Barassi, Super Coach of North Melbourne, be very, very worried—Collingwood is going to win this!

The halftime siren sounds.

SCENE TWO: THE 1977 GRAND FINAL HALF-TIME SPEECH

Lights change to give a bright light aura outline to a man standing in the doorway—the stadium behind him. He is in a sapphire blue suit and a light blue wide-collared shirt with several buttons undone.

A large crowd is now calling out full belt.

CROWD: Barassi! Barassi! Barassi Barassi!

BARASSI *has the famous scowl. He closes the door and the noise of the crowd is muffled. He walks from downstage right.*

MELBA *claps and an image of the Melbourne Cricket Ground locker rooms floods the stage.*

BARASSI *stands still and looks at his players for some loaded moments.*

BARASSI: A few more minutes until our moment of truth. This is the end-of-the-road day for the loser and only three things will stop it being *our* end-of-the-road. Guts, Determination and Fear. Yes, fear. Fear of *losing*. Gentlemen—the 1977 flag is *in your hands*. Now, they... [*indicating the Collingwood locker rooms next door*] Collingwood have not gone through what we have. If ever there was a day to prove that North Melbourne is now a club that has finally arrived as a league *power*—as a league power—this is your day!

He eyeballs many of them.

I'm asking you for guts. Only a team with *guts* will take their place in history. Nobody in the history of our mighty game has ever won a premiership from this position! You will take your place in history as a team that won the premiership after playing five finals in a row. If *ever* there was a day for guts, this is it. And it's no good being determined if you still go out there and let them make the first move. We've got to make the first bloody move... and we've got to do it in the first 15 *minutes*! They will hammer into you... and you've got to be *determined* to come back *twice as bloody hard!*

He looks at the faces staring back at him.

I can see that some of you are down because you're sore, you've made mistakes and you've got all sorts of bloody things wrong... I *know*—because I've been there!

He walks towards the door.

And it's worth it.

He opens it slightly—the roar of the crowd enters the room.

He shuts the door. The room is quieter.

Here, you've got 100,000 people who are urging and putting energy back into you! Suck everything of it that you can *in* and then pump it out! My men—you can achieve miracles in this world. YOU CAN

BE BETTER THAN YOU ARE! If you bloody *want* to! If you want to *enough!* But now, this has gone past the stage of wanting—it's something you *have to do!* Because, take this from me, you won't be able to *live with yourself if you lose!*

MELBA: Time, coach.

BARASSI: [*urgently*] Today we build our game around attack. Go for broke! Put the pressure on through running and tackling, we'll carve this mob up! I want blokes chased and hammered into the ground! If we're not doing it, they'll be doing it to us. So it's going to get back to who does it first and who does it best. Guts. Determination. Fear!

MELBA: They gotta go out now, coach.

BARASSI: [*screaming now*] I want the North Melbourne heat turned on! I want them fried by the heat! I want fried Magpie, fried Magpie's what I want for my supper and it'll go beautifully with champagne! Follow your captain David out *there* and take that bloody mob apart!

The siren sounds.

MELBA *adjusts the scoreboard:*
Collingwood 19.10.124, North Melbourne 21.25.151

MELBA *reluctantly waves the* ENSEMBLE *to sing the North Melbourne Football Club victory song.*

She stops them after a couple of lines. They all stare at her.

MELBA: You only know you are a true Collingwood supporter—

ENSEMBLE 3: When one of your kids was born on a pool table?

MELBA: When love for your club is tested and you stay true!

ENSEMBLE 2: When you think Dom Perignon is a Mafia boss?

MELBA: Barassi tested my love over and over.

ENSEMBLE 1: Or when you think the loaded dishwasher means your wife is drunk?

MELBA: Barassi was Collingwood's *formidable* enemy. When he joined North Melbourne they were the cellar dwellers, the easy-beats, the wooden spooners of the league.

ENSEMBLE 1 & 3: [*together*] Like the Dees now.

ENSEMBLE 2: Yeah, rub it in!

MELBA: In two short years Barassi coached, conspired and coerced—catapulting the League's weaklings into their first ever Grand Final victory. In 1975, while the Hawks wept, the joyous cries of the North Melbourne supporters could be heard on the moon.

She snaps her fingers and the ENSEMBLE *begin to sing the North Melbourne Football Club song once more.*

MELBA *snaps her fingers to make them stop.*

So while Barassi broke Collingwood supporters' hearts year after year, he taught us something precious about ourselves.

ENSEMBLE 1: What's got 100 legs and four teeth?

ENSEMBLE 3: Front row of the Collingwood Cheer Squad.

MELBA: [*to the audience*] Isn't it sad to see such envy in the young? [*To* ENSEMBLE] Listen and learn from history, cheeky fellas. This is your story too! A Melbourne story of a home-grown legend that begins in 1940.

SCENE THREE: 1940, BARASSI SENIOR JOINS UP

MELBA *waves as if she is conducting and 1940s music begins.*

She claps her hands and images of the 1940s flood the stage, stopping at an image of Sir Robert Menzies.

MELBA: This man is our Prime Minister. To celebrate coming out of decades of Depression, Melbourne has fallen in love with the King of Swing!

She clicks her fingers and Swing music begins. MELBA *then touches the shoulder of one of the* ENSEMBLE *and he dances the swing—a woman,* ENSEMBLE 4, *joins him—they dance.*

Melbourne boogie woogies and jives!

They boogie woogie and jive.

Then we Lindy Hop our way right into the Second World War!

The DANCERS *dance off.*

The Swing music changes into marching.

Nearly a million Australians join the military.

The marching segues into a war-time Vera Lynne song.

MELBA *snaps her fingers and a headline is seen:*

SLIDE: 'THE ARGUS:
  AUSTRALIA AT WAR
  WITH ITALY'

When Australia declares war on Italy. Every Aussie with a surname that finished in a vowel is given a hard time—including our hero's father.

RON BARASSI SENIOR *(26 years old) enters, wearing a 1940 Melbourne Football Club outfit. He is wearing the number 31.*

SENIOR: Norm! Norm! Over here!

SENIOR *is jumping up and down and* MELBA *circles him.*

MELBA: Ron Barassi Senior has just played for Melbourne in the Grand Final with his good friend Norm Smith.

SENIOR: Get your skates on, Norm!

MELBA: Barassi's father looks very much like his son. Sooo handsome with those cheeky dimples.

She flicks his cheek. SENIOR *thinks it's a fly as he calls out to* NORM:

SENIOR: Over here!

MELBA: Melbourne Football Club recruited him from country Victoria and found him a job at the Melbourne City Council.

SENIOR *backs up into the stage and lines up to take a mark. He takes a chest mark.*

Enter Norm Smith.

NORM SMITH *(25 years old) runs on.*

It is commonly believed that Melbourne Football Club was full of toffs, but Norm Smith—its most famous son—was the son of an ironmonger.

The two men are wearing medals around their necks.

NORM: No chest marks, Barassi—you lose too much time.

SENIOR *handballs it to him.*

Handball with your left to hit the target to your right.

SENIOR: You're not the bloody coach yet, Norm.

MELBA: As a kid Norm was a mad Magpie supporter but was zoned to play for Melbourne.

They tackle and SENIOR *gets the ball.*

SENIOR: You might look like Tarzan but you're playing like Jane!

NORM *gets it off him again and they fall in a heap on the ground laughing. They lie on their backs and look at the sky and sigh in a joint happiness. Then giggle again at their mutual exhilaration.*

SENIOR *sits up.*

This would have to be one of the best days of my life.

NORM *sits up.*

NORM: 70,000 people.

SENIOR: 35,000 of 'em want to buy you a beer and the other 35 want to cut your heart out!

NORM: It's the best feeling in the world.

SENIOR *uses this opportunity to nick the ball off* NORM.

As the boys tackle, a TELEGRAM BOY *rides by on a bicycle.*

The men become still.

MELBA: In wartime, telegram boys were both loved and dreaded. The messages they carried could be news of their loved ones coming home on leave, or news that their loved ones were never coming home; not even in a wooden box.

NORM: Hope he's not going to Cliff's house.

SENIOR: When did Cliffy sign up?

NORM: No, no, he's ridden past.

The men relax again.

MELBA: Enter Elza Barassi.

A woman in a 1940s outfit enters.

She married the handsome rover six years before in 1935 when she was 19.

ELZA *approaches the boys with Senior's military uniform.* SENIOR *takes it off her and pulls the trousers on.*

NORM: Hey, Elza—where's little Ronny?

ELZA: He was so tired that Carlo had to carry him to bed.

NORM: Little Ronny told Marj the other day that when he grows up he is going to…

ELZA: [*often quoted*] … play in a Grand Final like his dad.

NORM: That's right, play in a Grand Final like his dad, but listen to this: *retire* at 45.

ELZA: 45?

SENIOR: My boy said that?

NORM: Marj is still cracking up about it.

MELBA: Marj is Norm's fiancée.

SENIOR: Planning his retirement and he's just a kid.

ELZA: So are you.

SENIOR: Steady on, love.

ELZA: They're a good length. I've done the arms well.

NORM: Bit short, were we, Ron?

SENIOR: Don't want to be chasing Jerry and be tripping over me cuffs.

> SENIOR *puts on the jacket.*

ELZA: How is Marj?

NORM: She's hoping Ron will be back for our wedding.

SENIOR: That will all depend on the opposing team.

NORM: Let's hope their form drops like Richmond did today!

SENIOR: How do I look?

> SENIOR *is in uniform and* ELZA *leans up against* NORM. *They both say nothing as the reality of what* SENIOR *will become hits them.*

Not that bad, is it?

ELZA: Carlo had a dream.

SENIOR: C'mon, love. Don't start.

NORM: How is your dad?

SENIOR: Dad got a bee in his bonnet.

ELZA: Carlo's upset.

SENIOR: He gets too emotional.

NORM: Must be that Italian blood.

SENIOR: Dad is as Aussie as you are.

NORM: I'm well aware of / that, mate!

SENIOR: He'd sign up himself if he wasn't too old.

NORM: I'd sign up if they'd bloody well let me.

ELZA: Carlo dreamt that Ron wasn't coming back.

Pause.

SENIOR: Hey, I dreamt that I would kick eight bloody goals in the Grand Final but it was Smithy here who did that.

NORM: Seven goals.

SENIOR: You were robbed. That was your goal—not Baggot's.

NORM: I gotta get back. I just wish. I wish I was going with you.

ELZA: You're Essential Services.

NORM: Essential? Why do I feel so useless… pointless?

SENIOR: The country would fall apart without engineers—it'll cope without me, without flippin' council workers!

ELZA: My brother is coming over—he'd love to see you, Norm.

NORM: I promised I'd meet Marj. [*He hesitates.*] Ron—I'll see you? I'll see you again.

SENIOR: Sure you will, mate—don't be a galah.

ELZA: Might even be back for your wedding.

SENIOR: Keep an eye on young Ronny, will you?

NORM: I will.

SENIOR: If—

NORM: I'll look after him.

SENIOR: Sure you will. You know he's a stubborn little mite. Don't let him get too big for his boots.

> SENIOR *holds out his hand and* NORM *goes to shake but* SENIOR *puts his hand up to scratch his face just before* NORM*'s hand reaches his.* NORM *laughs—it's an old handshake gag joke.* SENIOR *then hugs* NORM *hard.*

> SENIOR *and* ELZA *exit hand in hand and* NORM *is left on his own watching his best friend walk off.*

SCENE FOUR: TOBRUK

Sounds of World War Two fighter planes.

MELBA *hands military clothes to two* ENSEMBLE MEMBERS.

MELBA: Scene Four. Tobruk, Libya, Northern Africa—the other side of the world from the muddy ovals where Ronald James Barassi would train after work at the Melbourne City Council.

SENIOR *climbs tentatively out of a hole. He takes his helmet off. He is without his shirt. It's hot and dry. He ties a hanky on his head while shooing away flies as he makes a football out of bits of canvas.*

Another SOLDIER*'s head pops up.*

SOLDIER 1: [*English accent*] That's not a ball, Barassi.

SENIOR: Hey, I'll bet you your next consignment of ciggies that I can kick this and hit the dunny door.

SOLDIER 1: [*English accent*] Dunny?

Another SOLDIER *pops up warily.*

SOLDIER 2: [*Australian accent*] Don't bet with that soldier—he plays for the top side back in Melbourne.

An explosion sounds off and they all pop down again.

When the noise clears all three pop up again.

SOLDIER 1: Australian Rules is a strange little sport, sport!

SENIOR: It's the sport of sports, sport!

SOLDIER 2: Face it, Barassi, it'll die out.

SENIOR: Spoken like a true New South Welshman.

SOLDIER 2: A 'Barassilini' should be playing soccer.

SENIOR: I'm Australian as a dunny door so you can stick your Pommy sport up your Khyber Pass.

SENIOR *kicks the ball and it falls apart. The other men laugh and* SENIOR *joins in.*

OFFICER IN CHARGE: Bill Grogan's been on supply mission for nine nights in a row. I need a volunteer to relieve him. Who's up for driving his truck tonight?

SENIOR: I'll do it—to get away from these bloody rugby lovers.

The OFFICER IN CHARGE *and* SENIOR *walk away. The heads pop down. The desert is quiet.*

In the distance there is the sound of a bomb being dropped.

MELBA *solemnly puts a* POST BOY*'s hat on an* ENSEMBLE *member.*

SLIDE: An image of a house in Footscray, 1941

The POST BOY *rides to Elza's brother's house. He gets off his bike and goes in.* MELBA *quotes from the poem 'Vitae Summa Brevis' by Ernest Dowson:*

MELBA: 'Out of a misty dream
Our path emerges for a while, then closes
Within a dream.'

> *The* POST BOY *comes back out looking grim. He gets on his bicycle and rides off.* ELZA *staggers out. She stands silently, looking at the telegram.*

> NORM *enters and rushes to* ELZA, *rocking her back and forth.*

You know the soldier that Ron Senior relieved—Bill Grogan? He lived for another 63 years.

ELZA: What's going to become of him, Norm? What's going to become of our little boy?

> *They hold each other for a moment as Billy Holiday sings 'God Bless the Child'.*

> ELZA *breaks from* NORM *still holding the telegram.*

What will become of my boy?

SCENE FIVE: WHAT WILL BECOME OF RONNY?

Music: 1950s pop song twang.

MELBA *places an old-fashioned metal bin strategically on stage.*

A big bullock of a boy enters. It is 14-year-old BARASSI. *He has a football and is concentrating so hard that he knocks over the bin.*

NORM *and* JACK MUELLER *are watching.*

NORM: Jeeeeesus, Ronny.
BARASSI: Sorry, Norm.
NORM: Right. I've told Jack here that you've got a good kick. Don't let me down.
BARASSI: I'm the biggest kick in the street, Mr Mueller.
NORM: Well, you show him, okay?

> NORM *throws him the ball.* BARASSI *trips over his feet again dropping the ball.*

Jesus!

BARASSI *with steely determination slowly backs out of view.*

MELBA: This is Melbourne's seconds coach Jack Mueller who also played with Ron's dad.

She picks up the man's gloved hand.

He lost two fingers in a carton-cutting machine at work but continued to play with a glove on. He was called The Hun on account of his German background. Jack tried to enlist at the same time as Ron Senior. The military rejected him on account of his injuries, which is kinda funny when the man went on to be a leading goalkicker, playing in both the 1940 and '41 premierships.

BARASSI *has backed all the way offstage but falls over something.*

The sounds of the crash make the two men frown.

MUELLER: This better be worth my Saturday, Norm!

NORM: [*to* BARASSI, *offstage*] Okay, kick it like I showed you.

We hear the thwack of the ball being kicked. The men's heads shoot across—the ball has gone a long way away.

MUELLER: Where is he living?

NORM: Brunswick.

BARASSI *runs back across stage to go and fetch the ball.*

MUELLER: So that means he's zoned?

NORM: For Carlton or / Collingwood.

MUELLER: Carlton?

NORM: I'm afraid.

MUELLER: A Barassi playing for Carlton? Should be a law against it.

NORM: I'm working on it.

BARASSI *runs back in with the ball.*

Tell Jack what you are going to do when you grow up, Ronny.

BARASSI: Play for Melbourne in a Grand Final.

MUELLER: Just like your dad.

BARASSI: Just like my dad.

MUELLER: Show us your kick again.

NORM: Aim for the cat on the Hendersons' lawn.

He backs out again and again kicks.

MUELLER: Oooh—ugly kick.

> BARASSI *kicks it to the other side of the ground.*

But, my Lord!

> *Again* NORM *and* MUELLER'*s heads shoot across from one side to the other.*

> *There is a painful meow. The two men make their way to the Hendersons.*

NORM: We gotta fight for the father/son rule to bring him to Melbourne.

MELBA: And they did. Barassi was cleared to join his father's club.

ENSEMBLE 2: So Barassi would have played for Collingwood?

MELBA: Do you know how much that keeps me awake at night? Thinking what if? What if Barassi had played for the Pies?!

SCENE SIX: AVENUE OF HONOUR

The stage is filled with trees lined in an avenue of honour. Some of the trees are soldiers with branches sticking out of them.

MELBA: Barassi would walk to primary school every day under a grove of trees that were planted by the road in his father's honour.

> BARASSI *is handballing the ball in the air. He catches it over and over. He is obsessive and devotional.*

> MELBA *walks around him as he practises.*

And now he was practising every day to be just like him. A champion football player.

> BARASSI *has the ball on his own, practising imaginary baulks in between the avenue of dead soldiers.*

> *Music: Eddie Fisher sings 'I'm Walking Behind You'.*

SCENE SEVEN: TAS-BLOODY-MANIA

MELBA: But his dreams to follow in his father's footsteps could be crushed. His mother, Elza, after 11 years working two jobs to raise the boy on her own, finds love again.

She gestures to an ENSEMBLE MEMBER.

Come here.

MELBA *places some old-fashioned Clark Kent glasses on the* ENSEMBLE MEMBER*'s face*

Remember, he doesn't get sarcasm. [*To the audience*] Enter the affable but earnest Colin Brewster.

The ENSEMBLE MEMBER *becomes* COLIN BREWSTER.

COLIN: [*to* BARASSI] Life is a series of sacrifices.

MELBA: Elza's new husband Colin lived 400 miles away from his father's beloved Melbourne Football Club.

NORM *and* ELZA *catch up to* COLIN.

NORM: [*to* BARASSI] Have you been practising?

BARASSI *nods his head.*

COLIN: Practising? The boy doesn't stop practising. I tell his mother—the boy needs to come inside sometimes—relax, listen to the wireless like other kids; it can't be good for him.

NORM *nods to* BARASSI *who runs backwards (offstage) to line up his kick.*

ELZA: He's not taking the news well.

COLIN: The boy has to learn that life is a series of sacrifices.

NORM: [*to* BARASSI] Aim for the bin next to the seesaw.

COLIN: His father understood sacrifice.

There is a thwack of a boot hitting leather and ELZA, COLIN *and* NORM *all rapidly turn their heads to watch the football fly with extraordinary velocity across the park. The ball lands with a clatter in a metal bin.*

ELZA: Ugly kick.

NORM: But, by jingo, it's accurate.

COLIN: His father made the ultimate sacrifice.

NORM: We fought so hard…

ELZA: Yes.

NORM: … so we wouldn't lose him…

COLIN: Sacrificed his life.

ELZA: Yes.

NORM: … to Collingwood…

ELZA: Yes.

NORM: … or even worse Carlton—

ELZA: Norm—

NORM: But Tas-bloody-mania?!

> MELBA *clicks her fingers and the vision of a hut in the Tasmanian wilderness appears.*

ELZA: It's not that I'm not grateful / for all…

COLIN: It's the boy who should be grateful, his mother's worked two jobs to raise him, she knows sacrifice and so should the boy.

> BARASSI *skulks across the stage to retrieve the ball—clearly gloomy.*

ELZA: I know it's breaking his heart.

NORM: It's breaking my bloody heart.

ELZA: But he needs to be with his mother.

COLIN: And a wife needs to be with her husband—it's sacrifice—we, of all people know about sacrifice, don't we, Norm?

NORM: I didn't serve, Colin.

COLIN: My mistake.

> *The ball flies back in to hit* COLIN.

ELZA: Ronny!

> BARASSI *runs in clearly impressed with his shot.*

COLIN: [*admiringly*] You're stepping into your dad's footsteps, Ronny.

BARASSI: Then I'd better biff you over the head seeing you're sleeping with his wife.

ELZA: I'll biff you, Ronny, in a minute.

BARASSI: Have you asked her, Norm? What'd she say?

NORM: 'She' is the cat's mother, Ron.

ELZA: Ask me what?

BARASSI: We can't move to Tasmania, Mum.

COLIN: A wife has to move to where her husband works, son.

BARASSI: I'm not your son.

COLIN: I'm well aware of that, son. It's a figure of speech.

ELZA: Norm, a 16-year-old needs his mother.

BARASSI: So stay in Brunswick.

COLIN: What's the fuss? The boy could join a team in Tasmania.

BARASSI: And I could join a crochet group while I'm at it. Col.

ELZA: Ronny. That's enough from you.

BARASSI: [*whining*] Mum, I don't want—

ELZA: One more word, Ronny!

NORM: Tasmania would never release him to Melbourne. Once he plays for them he'll never play for his father's team.

ELZA: But Ronny can't live on his own. What with me working all the time the boy has spent too long on his own as it is.

BARASSI: I don't mind being on my own, Mum.

NORM: I've talked to Marj and we think Ron could move in with us.

ELZA: You've no room.

NORM: We'll build a bungalow out the back; give the lad some privacy.

BARASSI: Mum, I'll visit you all the time.

COLIN: And if the boy isn't any good he can come and live with us.

BARASSI: [*sarcastic*] Thanks, Col.

COLIN: [*oblivious*] That's alright, boy, you'll always be welcome at the Brewster home.

ELZA: You want to live away from me, Ronny?

BARASSI: No, Mum… no, I…

ELZA: Good. Then it's settled then. He finishes his schooling in Tasmania.

BARASSI: Mum!

ELZA: It's my final word.

> BARASSI *backs out again into the wings.*

COLIN: The boy won't be able to kick the ball against the garage wall all morning before school the way he does at your place. I've got those roses my mother planted.

> *We hear the thwack of his boot on the leather—the three heads again fly across as they watch the certain trajectory of the ball that lands with a clutter into the metal rubbish bin.*

> MELBA *brings out the bin and shows the audience the ball inside it.*

MELBA: [*in a parody of contemporary slang*] Skills!

> BARASSI *begins to walk back in again. He looks pleadingly at his mother.*

ELZA: I'll pay for the bungalow to be built and Ronny will pay board.

> BARASSI *runs and hugs* ELZA, *picking her up and spinning her around.*

BARASSI: You'll watch me play for Melbourne like you watched Dad play for Melbourne!

ELZA: You can put me down now.

BARASSI: I'll pay for your ferry from Tassie!

ELZA: Go and get the ball.

> *As* BARASSI *runs off to get the ball,* ELZA, *a proud woman, tries to hold back her tears.*

COLIN: She worked like a slave all her life for that boy—getting half the salary of a man for the same work. But, I always say, you have to pay the same at the butcher's for your chop— / man or woman.

ELZA: Col.

MELBA: I'm with Col here.

NORM: I'll build the bungalow, Elza.

COLIN: Now, I'm no woman's libber, but a woman's bills aren't cut in half, so why is her pay?

MELBA: Here, bloody here!

ELZA: Col. Be quiet! [*To* NORM] I'll pay for the materials.

COLIN: But you've got me now, love.

NORM: Your lad will be well looked after.

> BARASSI *runs back in with the ball.*

COLIN: And he'll have a better crack at getting a match living with the coach.

SCENE EIGHT: LIVING WITH THE COACH

The sounds of a modest football crowd.

BARASSI *handballs it to a* PLAYER *who is tackled so he quickly handballs it back to him but* BARASSI *falls over himself and loses possession.*

PLAYER 1: You're only getting a match because you live with the coach.

> *SLIDE: Image of the Melbourne Cricket Ground, circa 1953*

MELBA: Ron Barassi continued to play under the watchful eye of seconds coach Jack Mueller.

NORM and MUELLER *are looking at the players.*

Two young PLAYERS *line up for a mark when a barrelling* BARASSI *smashes through and they lay dazzled on the ground.*

MUELLER *checks the eyeballs of one of the players, then slaps his face. He pushes him back out into the field.*

MUELLER: Barassi's kid is useless to me, Norm. I put him forward, I've tried him back, he's a bloody disaster—he's all arms 'n' legs 'n' it's like a crosswired torpedo—but it's his teammates he's tumbling while the ball keeps disappearing back up the ground.

The PLAYERS *go to mark again and again* BARASSI *dives in and they all tumble away.* BARASSI *gets straight up and chases the ball. A* PLAYER *gets up dazed.*

PLAYER 2: Coach! You gotta get that kid off the ground before he kills us all.

The other PLAYERS *stand up and* BARASSI *comes running back on like a rambunctious overgrown puppy.*

PLAYER 3: [*snidely to* BARASSI] Hey, Muscle-inny. Do us a favour and go back to Eye-tie land.

BARASSI *smiles a gap-toothed smile and they push him over.*

MUELLER: He hasn't got the size or the skill to hold down a senior position.

BARASSI *stands up, has a shake and runs off unruffled.*

NORM: He's so much like his dad.

MUELLER: It's like Ronald James didn't get old.

NORM: He didn't get old like we've got old.

MUELLER: You know I dream of Ron some nights.

NORM: So do I.

MUELLER: He's back from the war, he's alive.

NORM: Hurts to wake up.

MUELLER: In the dream, he's always laughing.

NORM: Ron loved a laugh.

MUELLER: He hated losing at anything.

NORM: Just like his son.

MUELLER: Alright. What about we play Ronny on the back line?

Lights shift on ELZA *in Tasmania, scouring the paper for news of her son.*

SCENE NINE: TASMANIA 1

While ELZA *is looking through the Melbourne papers,* BARASSI *is running on the spot with a house brick in each hand.*

ELZA: Col! Col! Look here. It's Ron—look.

COLIN: [*reading from the paper*] 'The five foot ten-and-a-half inches son of the former Melbourne champion killed in the war showed great dash on the back line.' [*Putting the paper down*] That's very good, love.

ELZA: [*taking the paper*] They've spelt his name wrong.

COLIN: At least you don't have that problem anymore, now do you, Mrs Brewster? Now where's that dinner, ay?

Lights down on Tasmania.

SCENE TEN: NUMBER 31

MELBA: Melbourne Cricket Ground, 1950s.

MELBA *clicks her fingers and we see an image of the MCG in the 1950s.*

NORM *enters with a jumper.*

NORM: Ronny!

BARASSI *runs in again and trips but manages to not fall down.*

BARASSI: I've been working on my follow-through; see. I practise before school.

NORM: Yes, you wake me and Marj up.

BARASSI *prepares to kick.*

Jack and I have been talking.

BARASSI *is distracted and trips himself up and falls down.*

BARASSI: I'll just do that again.

NORM: Here look—

He hands BARASSI *the jumper. On the back is the number 31.*

You can play in it on Saturday.

BARASSI *can't speak he's so touched.*

NORM *smiles and walks away.*

BARASSI *holds the jumper close to him.*

The far-off sounds of a big band of the 1940s: Glenn Miller's 'Elmer's Tune'.

BARASSI *holds the jumper out and has a tiny dance. It is as if he is dancing with his dad. His dance isn't awkward, it's nearly graceful.*

The music and the dance stop when NORM *comes in with a* PHOTOGRAPHER *who takes a photo.*

ANOTHER PHOTOGRAPHER *comes in and* BARASSI *poses with the jumper. He puts the jumper on.*

The sounds of a crowd... and BARASSI *runs out to play.*

SCENE ELEVEN: TASMANIA 2

MELBA: Tasmania.

COLIN *is reading a Victorian newspaper while* ELZA *proudly watches.*

COLIN: 'Demons have hope for Ron Barassi the second. 17-year-old Ron Barassi who has won his way on to Melbourne's final training list, will wear 31, his late father's number.'

ELZA: Look. He's photographed under all his father's trophies.

COLIN: That's very good, love.

ELZA: I'm going to cut it out.

COLIN: You'll ruin the paper.

ELZA: I'm going to cut it out and start a scrapbook.

SCENE TWELVE: OUR MATE'S SON IS BLOODY USELESS

Sounds of an umpire's whistle.

MELBA *runs on as an umpire in full white attire.* BARASSI *runs back. He goes to the front of the stage, breathing heavily and very annoyed with himself. Melbourne* SUPPORTERS *sitting in the auditorium sit up in their seats and call out to him in anger:*

SUPPORTER 1: You're not half the footballer your dad was.

SUPPORTER 2: Take off that guernsey! Barassi, take off that guernsey!

SUPPORTER 3: You're not number 31 and you never will be!

> BARASSI *is astonished and hurt. He runs off.*

> MUELLER *and* NORM *have been watching.*

MUELLER: Gotta face it, Norm. Our mate's son is bloody useless. He won't stay in position.

NORM: The boy just needs to run. I've never seen a player so determined to get the ball.

MUELLER: So you're suggesting rover?

NORM: No, not rover.

MUELLER: 'Cause he's too big to rove.

NORM: In the ruck.

MUELLER: He's not big enough to ruck.

NORM: He'll be second ruck.

MUELLER: Second rucks need to be even bigger for the knockouts / Cordner...

NORM: Was McPherson big enough? He and Don Cordner made a winning combination in '48.

MUELLER: I dunno, Norm—the boy is a pain in the arse.

NORM: So were you, Jack. Biggest pain in the arse in the VFL. Ronny!

> BARASSI *runs on. He's running on the spot. He then does two-arm push-ups, then one-arm push-ups. He's fit, he's keen and he's anxious that he's about to be dropped.*

[*To* MUELLER] Cordner doesn't need help with the knockouts—but Ron can be his backup. Christ, here am I trying to curb his bloody enthusiasm. I need him to run, pick up the spills, be free to rove.

MUELLER: [*irritated*] But we have Spencer as rover.

NORM: He'll be backup to Spencer.

MUELLER: A ruck that's free to rove.

NORM: Or a rover that plays in the ruck.

BARASSI: Coach? Jack? Norm? Just tell me. Tell me.

NORM: We want you in the ruck—you're second ruck to Cordner—and you support the rover. Let Cordner do most of the tap work.

MUELLER: And for God's sake, keep out of his way.

BARASSI *grins a gap-toothed smile and shoots off.*

Music: 'Oop Shoop' by The Crew Cuts.

MELBA: Barassi ran out on the field like a colt out of the barriers—the ball and only the ball was he chasing and at last he was free to go anywhere on the ground.

SCENE THIRTEEN: A RUCK ROVER IS BORN

SLIDE: Melbourne Cricket Ground

A gabardine-coated NORM *steps out in front of his players.*

NORM: We are making football faster—I want the ball moving down the oval faster, we must handball more, always be looking out for each other. Football is changing and because of this faster pace, sides must have a mobile ruck team and it is here that young Barassi is most valuable—he will skirt the fringe of the packs, aid the rover to dispose of the ball or get it himself. The ruck rover is our All Bran—designed to eliminate congestion. Spencer and Cordner… keep Barassi at your disposal—be alert to his presence at all times.

BARASSI *runs on—he has had his teeth pulled out and isn't wearing his false teeth. He hisses to* SPENCER *but it is barely understandable.*

BARASSI: Spencer here, here!

SPENCER *is being tackled so he handballs to* BARASSI—*the opposition chase* BARASSI *who expertly handballs back to* SPENCER.

MELBA: Tassie.

SCENE FOURTEEN: TASMANIA 3

ELZA: Col! Listen to this. [*Reading from her scrapbook*] From the *Herald*. 'Barassi shone in the ruck'. The *Sun*—'Barassi capably played the part of ruckman rover'. Then in the *Sporting Globe*. 'Barassi used as rover ruckman'. Col—are you there, love? [*She reads wistfully from her clippings.*] 'He showed courage and dash, and was playing strongly at the finish.'

MELBA: As Elza reads her scrapbook in sleepy Tasmania, the Red Legs have lost and Norm is on the rampage.

As MELBA *snaps her fingers the stage becomes the locker rooms at the MCG.*

SCENE FIFTEEN: WRATH OF NORM SMITH

PLAYERS *gather around* NORM *who is giving* BARASSI *a spray. The other* PLAYERS *bow their heads.*

NORM: There are 17 other blokes out there slaving their guts out for the team, yet here you are—you play on, you bloody play on—you could've handballed it to Dixon or Beckwith but you didn't. You've let the whole side down! You let them down! You may be named best bloody player in the papers but I'm here to tell you you're not. You're nothing to me if you don't play in a team! We were two points behind and you should have handballed but no, no, you bounced and you were baulked and you were caught! If you weren't so bloody selfish, so bloody selfish! [*His eyes are flashing a deep anger.*] You know your father won Most Unselfish Player—you know that, well what would he think about you losing the game today because you wanted to shoot for goal?—you wanted to be the bloody hero, the newspaper's best boy. This was too big a match and too much bloody at stake to bloody be like that. You lost us the game today, Ronny. You lost us the game.

NORM *exits.*

A PLAYER *tousles* BARASSI'*s hair trying to make him feel better.* BARASSI *is near tears.* MELBA *gives him some boots and a cloth to clean them with.*

SCENE SIXTEEN: ELZA VISITS HER SON

BARASSI *is cleaning his footy boots.*

ELZA *enters, reading quotes from newspaper clippings as she approaches.*

ELZA: 'Inspirational, the best ruck in the game.'

BARASSI: Don't let Norm hear this.

ELZA: 'He swung opponents around like a bag of onions.'

BARASSI: Mum, stop.

ELZA: 'Scorns personal safety'—now that's my boy!

BARASSI: [*concerned that* NORM *will hear*] Really, shush, stop.

ELZA: You shush! Round two he was a 'go-through artist'. [*Looking up*] An artist! [*She giggles.*] They're calling you 'an artist!'.

He tries to take the scrap book from her but she dodges him.

[*Continuing to quote*] 'Outstanding aerial skills', 'fearless', 'a headache'.

BARASSI: A headache? Where'd they say that?

ELZA: Here—look at that picture. You should keep your teeth in, Ronny.

BARASSI: It scares the opponents if I take me falsies out.

ELZA: If you'd brushed your teeth like I told you!

BARASSI *reads through the clippings.*

BARASSI: Yeah, well too late now.

ELZA: Was heavy lugging that thing on the boat.

BARASSI: Thanks for this, Mum.

ELZA: Col says hello.

BARASSI: Right.

ELZA: Wish your father could see you now.

BARASSI: You know sometimes—wearing his number, 31—it feels as if Dad is still out on the field. I think that his number helps me when the going is rugged.

ELZA *is moved by this.*

You okay, Mum?

ELZA: You love playing as much as he did.

BARASSI: There's nothing like it. You know journalists, they ask me what's it like out on the field in a final, and I stumble over the words, like I used to stumble over the ball—I have so much to say…

ELZA: I know you do.

BARASSI: … but I end up sounding like an idiot. I want to answer their questions but I…

ELZA: Tell me.

BARASSI: What?

ELZA: Describe to me what is it like to play in a Grand Final.

BARASSI: It's aaaaah— [*lost for words*] indescribable!

ELZA: Ronny, you can do it—just go back in your mind to the Grand Final and describe it to me. One word at a time. Okay?

BARASSI: I can't.

ELZA: The siren sounds.

BARASSI: Mum.

ELZA: Close your eyes and hear the siren

> BARASSI *closes his eyes.*

> *We hear a siren.*

BARASSI: Siren—

ELZA: What do you do?

BARASSI: [*eyes still closed*] You run onto the ground of course.

ELZA: Look! Take this seriously.

BARASSI: Okay, Mum.

> *The sounds of a crowd.*

You feel the chill in the air, the wet grass under your feet and...

ELZA: Go on.

BARASSI: ... it's bloody cold, you know.

ELZA: Don't swear, Ronny, but go on!

BARASSI: Sorry, Mum. It's cold, but I've got Dad's number on my back and the crowd is like a blanket of... you feel them, you feel them all...

> *'Screaming', 'crying out', 'encouraging'—he struggles to put the words in the right place.*

ELZA: Go on—don't stop, one word, then the next word; you're the best person in the world to tell us this.

BARASSI: The crowd, so loud. You have to scream for your teammates to hear. The centre bounce, and that's it—the ball, the ball—you feel the crowd willing the ball to come to you, to come to you! And when it does, when the ball flies through the air straight at you—the surge, the hope—the thrill when you know that the ball is yours; in that moment in time you fly, Mum, you fly and your hands...

> *He clasps her hands.*

… in your hands, is all this power, you have seconds, not even seconds to run, handball or kick—you live for that moment of possession. You have all this blood pumping through your veins and the crowd, thousands of hearts pumping their blood, bursting their hearts for you to move that ball into the precise place for our victory.

He holds her hand and pulls his mother around the room.

You're holding on to all their dreams, in those few seconds you are in control of the hopes of thousands of dreams. We are all together, wishing all for one thing—that those seconds unite us and we win, we win the flag!

ELZA: Bravo, Ronny!

BARASSI: But I wouldn't blab on like that to the *Herald*.

ELZA: Maybe you should.

BARASSI: People think I'm up myself already.

ELZA: Nonsense—well, maybe sometimes you are.

BARASSI: Mum!

MELBA: Elza is bursting with pride but she won't show it, after all— it's the '50s, and in Australia getting too big for your boots—is the greatest social crime of all.

ELZA: How does that lovely girlfriend of yours feel about coming second to football?

BARASSI: Aaw, Nancy's a real good sort.

ELZA: Hope you're doing the right thing by her.

BARASSI: I want to marry her.

ELZA: No. Ronny, no!

BARASSI: To do the right thing.

ELZA: She's not…? [pregnant]

BARASSI: No, Mum. No. Mum!

ELZA: Well, don't be stupid. I haven't heard such a stupid thing. Why would two kids like you get married?

BARASSI: Well, Norm says it will keep me focused on football.

ELZA: There's no-one else in Australia as focused on football than you are.

BARASSI: Norm said.

ELZA: Norm's not your father or your mother!

BARASSI: I know that.

ELZA: Good.

BARASSI: He just thinks it will settle me down.

ELZA: Nonsense.

BARASSI: There aren't a lot of girls like Nancy around.

ELZA: It's not about Nancy! I love Nancy, I do, but you're both kids.

BARASSI: You married Dad when you were 19.

ELZA: Look where that got me—raising a young boy on my own at 24.

BARASSI: Mum!

ELZA: It's too big a decision.

BARASSI: I'm ready to make it.

ELZA: Ron, it's the '50s—women can have careers—isn't Nancy studying engineering?

BARASSI: She'll keep studying and working—both of us will.

ELZA: And when the babies come?

BARASSI: That'll be down the track a bit.

ELZA: That's what we thought but you were a wedding night baby.

BARASSI: Mum!

ELZA: Marriage is not a game—there are no more Grand Finals to chase the next year if you lose.

BARASSI: We don't plan to ever lose the Grand Final, Mum.

ELZA: See… [*sighing*] you're just a kid

BARASSI: Kid!? I've played in three Grand Finals. I've started my own business. Mum, I'm 20 years old. I don't drink, smoke or gamble. I work so bloody hard.

ELZA: You swear! And you lose your temper.

BARASSI: Where'd I get that from?

ELZA: Maybe you need to go a bit wild. I don't know. Sew some wild thingy-me-jigs.

BARASSI: Oats. You mean oats—why? Mum, why? When I'm doing exactly what I've always dreamed I'd be doing? I'm living a dream. I'm living thousands of dreams.

ELZA: Wait at least another year.

SCENE SEVENTEEN: THE BRIEFEST HONEYMOON

Wedding bells.

NORM *steps in and throws confetti. He is overjoyed.*

Music: 'Here Comes the Bride'.

In the distance we see a bride in white.

BARASSI *hurriedly puts on a morning coat and walks towards her.*

PHOTOGRAPHERS *snap.*

Light change.

The noise of a crowd.

PLAYERS *surround* BARASSI *and rip off his coat.* NORM *turns on* BARASSI *in deep frustration.* BARASSI *is swiftly back in the spray.*

NANCY, *the bride, remains in the background looking hopeful.*

SCENE EIGHTEEN: BARASSI BACK IN THE SPRAY

NORM: Barassi, where were you? Where bloody were you? Spencer was looking for you and looking for you and you were behind your man— You have to go faster. Football is faster now—it's not an amateur sport. You're not bloody gentlemen players! I want men who'll go to war for me! And you, Hassa! What was that? You weak-gutted bastard! Get that jumper off and show these blokes your yellow belly and the yellow streak down your back! Now get back out there and bomb those bloody Bombers!

> BARASSI *and the other* PLAYERS *run out.*
>
> NANCY *is left in her bridal outfit, looking bewildered.*
>
> *The following Jack Dyer radio commentary is heard as* BARASSI *comes off the football field and undresses. He's muddy and exhausted and he has a wild look in his eyes.*

JACK DYER: [*voice on the radio*] I'm giving Barassi two and a half votes. One—for murdering the Bombers in one of the best single-handed efforts I've seen in years. Two—for his great teamwork, he knitted his side together in the third quarter with precision football—the nearest approach to copybook football we've seen for quite a while.

> *A* TRAINER *comes and redresses* BARASSI'*s finger bandages. The* TRAINER *gives him a drink of cordial.* BARASSI *remains, staring out, with a look of concentration.*

Half a vote—for putting a bit of fire into the game when it was necessary. He supplied the thrills. He really took the game right up to Essendon and 'grounded' the lot.

All the PLAYERS *and* BARASSI *run out back to the ground.*

The PLAYERS *run back in.*

SCENE NINETEEN: AS VICE-CAPTAIN

The PLAYERS *are all triumphant and a little tipsy.*

BARASSI *shifts into a euphoric mood. He runs to his young bride* NANCY *and kisses her before getting up to make a speech.*

BARASSI: I'd like to say a few words.
PLAYER 3: When did you ever have to ask to say a few words, Barass?
BARASSI: Now I'm vice-captain.
PLAYER 1: Vice-captain? I thought you were running the place.
BARASSI: That's our coach.
PLAYER 2: Thought you were the coach, Barass.
PLAYER 1: He acts like the coach on the field.
BARASSI: That our coach, Norm Smith.
PLAYER 3: The man who must be obeyed.
PLAYER 2: The man who's always bloody right.
PLAYER 1: The only man who can keep Barassi pegged.
BARASSI: [*good naturedly*] Get stuffed, alright! I want to say that Norm Smith is a prince, no, he is the king of all coaches!

>   *The men cheer.*

We're a young team, we lost so many players, but Norm—you got us to where we are now.
PLAYERS: [*together*] Winners!
PLAYER 1: The best team in the League!
BARASSI: You're fair and just.
PLAYER 4: Yeah, a fair bastard.
PLAYER 3: And just a—[*bleeped out*]
BARASSI: You've been hard on me.

>   *There is a silence—it's nearly awkward;* NORM *has been particularly hard on him.*

But you've pushed me to be better than I am.

PLAYER 1: And you push us to be—[*bleeped out*]

BARASSI: We're a team, alright! A bloody good team and let me say I'm proud to be part of a team that will make Norm Smith's name go down in football history! So, Norm…

> *He holds out his hand and walks towards* NORM. NORM *puts out his hand to be shaken but* BARASSI *goes past and shakes* NANCY's *hand and then hugs her and spins her around.*
>
> NORM *stands there, shaking his head.* BARASSI *then hugs* NORM *as well as* NANCY. *The* PLAYERS *all cheer.* NORM *is touched as well as very proud.*

SCENE TWENTY: OUR FIRST MEDIA STAR

MELBA: 1956. This man is our Prime Minister.

> *SLIDE: Image of Sir Robert Menzies*

And a big heavy box arrived in our country that changed our lounge rooms and lives forever. Television lured the young and the old—this magic square that shone out images of life beyond our lives. You'd see whole families in their PJs and dressing-gowns outside shop windows wherever they were sold.

> *A group of people in pyjamas and dressing-gowns gather around a box projecting light.*

Barassi began a football clinic segment on the 'Happy Hammond Show'—thousands of kids would religiously tune in every week. Preparing for this show not only gave him ideas in how to communicate the skills of the game but by wearing different footy jumpers each week he was creating a young legion of devoted fans from every football club.

> *Projected on a screen is* BARASSI (*in an Essendon jumper*). *We see him perform his footy show in black and white.*
>
> *On the screen, a confident, smiling* BARASSI *makes lines on a blackboard with chalk.*

BARASSI: [*on the screen*] So that means you'd need to kick it to this player. [*He marks the spot on the blackboard.*] Here.

BARASSI *seems to walk off the screen and onto the stage. He is soon surrounded by* AUTOGRAPH HUNTERS.

MELBA: Barassi is asked to endorse many products.

ENSEMBLE: [*together, sung*] 'Stop and think and always drink a pint of milk a day.'

VOICE-OVER: Wherever there's a champion, you'll find that milk's the drink. Do as the champions do, say…

BARASSI *is led from his fans. A* MAKE-UP WOMAN *takes off his jumper and someone else gives him the Melbourne jumper while she powders his nose. Someone else hands him a glass of milk.*

BARASSI: 'Make Mine Milk'.

The milk is whipped away and BARASSI *is now handed a cigarette. A* STAGEHAND *lights it and he coughs a lot.*

COMMERCIAL DIRECTOR: Try again.

He takes a puff but doesn't inhale.

BARASSI: The smooth taste of Turf.

COMMERCIAL DIRECTOR: Cut! That's good.

BARASSI *is cross-eyed with nausea from the smoke. He is given a pair of football boots.*

BARASSI: [*to the camera*] What the champions wear.

SCENE TWENTY-ONE: BARASSI'S GOLDEN ERA

Celebratory music.

MELBA: 1954 to 1964 was the golden era of the Melbourne Football Club and its leading man with matinee idol looks was Ronald Dale Barassi.

BARASSI *runs back on and handballs high and then runs past the* PLAYERS, *catches the ball and plays on.*

Barassi grew into his body just as the visionary Norm Smith's master plan bore its fruit. These ten years the Demons reached all ten finals. No fewer than eight Grand Finals to win six premierships.

There are crowd sounds as BARASSI *runs on. He catches a magnificent mark and then kicks. His iconic kick is photographed.*

SLIDE: The statue of Barassi in the Parade of Champions at the Melbourne Cricket Ground

SCENE TWENTY-TWO: 1958 GRAND FINAL

MELBA: Barassi's star shone bright in Norm's Smith firmament. Except in one year.

ENSEMBLE 2: [*to another* ENSEMBLE MEMBER] This'll be '58.

ENSEMBLE 1: Melba's finest moment.

ENSEMBLE 2: [*cheekily to* MELBA] Was this 1958, Melba?

ENSEMBLE 3: Watch her glow as she gloats.

MELBA: [*to the audience*] Every Magpie supporter of a certain age will tell you that 1958 was one of the best Grand Finals ever fought and won and I'll tell you why!

ENSEMBLE 3: Tell us why, Melba.

ENSEMBLE 1: Tell it like we've never heard it before.

MELBA: Melbourne won premierships in 1955, '56 and '57—winning the '58 flag meant they would equal Collingwood's proud record of winning four flags in a row from 1927 to '30.

She snaps her fingers and lightning strikes.

The sound of rain and thunderstorms.

The rain did not stop 80,000 of us making our way to the MCG for the 1958 Grand Final. [*She puts on a rain hat.*] Did you know that, per capita, the VFL Grand Finals drew greater crowds than any other game in the world?

Lightning crack.

On this stormy, stormy day the only team between the Demons and the immortality of equalling Collingwood in winning four flags in a row was... drum roll...

ENSEMBLE: [*together*] Collingwood!

The ENSEMBLE *put on Collingwood jumpers.*

MELBA: Hollywood couldn't have scripted it better, folks. Norm Smith wanted that record real bad and Collingwood? We, just as bad, wanted to keep our record! Enter Legendary Collingwood coach Alphonsius E 'Phonse' Kyne.

A lightning strike lights up on a gabardine-coated PHONSE KYNE.

KYNE: We are the men to decide if we want the Melbourne Football Club to equal our club winning four premierships in a row.

A lightning strike lights up on a gabardine-coated NORM SMITH.

NORM: In the mud and muck these Magpies will think they have it over us—we are more skilled and more cohesive but they are Collingwood!

KYNE: I want no dirty stuff…

NORM: They are fanatical!

KYNE: … but I want those Demons hounded back to hell.

NORM: And they will want to keep their record at all costs, at all costs.

KYNE: Niggle them…

NORM: The Collingwood fellas reckon they'll have us sucked in.

KYNE: … niggle them and niggle them.

NORM: Don't let it happen!

KYNE: Let the Demons retaliate.

NORM: If those maggies peck, do not peck back!

KYNE: Remember…

NORM: Remember…

NORM & KYNE: [*together*] … what is at stake today!

> *Lights down on* NORM.

KYNE: [*conspiratorially*] Weideman.

MELBA: Enter acting captain of Collingwood, Murray 'The Weed' Weideman.

KYNE: [*conspiratorially*] Harrison.

MELBA: Enter Collingwood ruckman, Barry 'Hooker' Harrison.

KYNE: Men…

> HARRISON *and* WEIDEMAN *learn forward to listen to their coach's secret instructions.*

[*Conspiratorially*] If you want to stop Melbourne, you must stop Barassi!

> *Lights on both coaches.*

NORM: Remember.

KYNE: Remember.

NORM & KYNE: [*together*] History is at stake today.

Lights down on the coaches as BARASSI *runs on.*

MELBA: Now due to a copyright violation—both clubs were forced to change their numbers. Barassi had to wear number two.

As MELBA *hands* BARASSI *the number two Melbourne jumper, he snatches it from her.*

Will he be Samson shorn of his golden locks?

He shakes his head, changes his number and runs off.

The sounds of a huge crowd.

BARASSI *runs into position for the ball.*

[*To* HARRISON] Call him Ape Head. He hates it.

HARRISON *shoulders* BARASSI'*s shoulder with a huge thwack.*

HARRISON: Hey, Ape Head!

While BARASSI *is distracted for a second.* WEIDEMAN *dives in and pushes* BARASSI.

BARASSI: Murray?

HARRISON: Hey, Ape Head!

BARASSI *turns to* HARRISON *in anger and* WEIDEMAN *pushes him again.* BARASSI *thumps* WEIDEMAN. WEIDEMAN *is down on the ground.*

MELBA, *as umpire, blows her whistle.* WEIDEMAN *is given the ball and plays on.* BARASSI *hangs his head and is furious.*

The siren sounds.

BARASSI *falls to the ground in misery.*

The crowd is cheering.

BARASSI *gets up and walks away to the sounds of thousands of fans singing the Collingwood victory song.*

MELBA *joins in the song.*

The song morphs into a 'Dance to the Bop'.

MELBA: Ah! Victory!

A DANCER *wearing a Collingwood scarf dances to the Bop with* MELBA.

She stops the dance, then looks solemnly at the audience.

But wherever there is victory, there is the vanquished biding their time.

SCENE TWENTY-THREE: 1960 HUMILIATION

SLIDES: Images of Melbourne in the '60s flood the stage.

MELBA: 1960. Yet again the Demons face the Pies in the Grand Final. Barassi is now captain. The Red Legs were merciless in their revenge against us—we only managed to kick two goals for the whole match.

> *Lights up on* NORM.

NORM: Why did you let them have those two goals? Collingwood didn't deserve those two goals!

> *A baby cries along with some magpies.*

MELBA: Our defeat in 1960 gave us the lowest Grand Final score in history. 1960 pierced something deep inside us—on September 25, 1960 you could hear the weeping of Magpies all across the city.

SCENE TWENTY-THREE: '62 AT HOME WITH THE BARASSI'S

SLIDE: Image of Sir Robert Menzies

MELBA: 1962—this man is still our Prime Minister.

> *The crying baby transforms into laughter.*

Australia enters the Vietnam War. And…

> BARASSI *walks in with the laughing baby.*

… Ron Barassi the third arrives in this world.

> *The baby is laughing as* BARASSI *swings him around and around. Until he puts his shoulder joint out.*

BARASSI: Nancy!

> NANCY *enters and takes the baby off him. He adjusts his arm and there is a clunk as he puts his shoulder joint back in.*

NANCY: Ouch!

BARASSI: Happens all the time now.

MELBA: The invincible force's body was ageing.

BARASSI: Where do you keep the tea towels, love?

NANCY: Why?

BARASSI: Photographer is coming to do an article.

NANCY: Here?

BARASSI: 'At home with the Barassis'.

NANCY: So just me and the kids, then?

BARASSI: Funny.

NANCY: Sometimes I buy the newspapers just to remind me of what my husband looks like...

BARASSI: I thought a shot of you washing and me drying dishes.

NANCY: ... and to find out where he is.

BARASSI: Where do you keep them?

NANCY: Same place for the last five years.

BARASSI: Nancy, I know I've got to learn to say no to people but how do I say no to the Royal Children's Hospital? Some of these kids are dying and they see their football hero... read this...

> *He shows her a letter.*

NANCY: [*reading letter as she rocks the baby*] 'Dear Mr Barassi, My son Neil was suffering from breathing difficulties, doctors were in fear for his life. He was in hospital when you visited the ward. After you left, he showed such remarkable improvement that he went home the following day and is now out in the backyard wearing his number 31...'

> *She stops reading, she kisses her baby then goes to touch her husband's cheek but he turns away to exit.*

Tea towels live in the third drawer down.

BARASSI: [*as he exits*] Next to the sink?

NANCY: By the stove.

> NANCY *rocks her baby and sings the Melbourne Football Club victory song to him.*

SCENE TWENTY-FOUR: THE BIG DECISION

MELBA: 1964: Judy Hanrahan becomes Australia's first female bank teller, the Beatles visit Australia, this man is our Prime Minister...

SLIDE: Image of Sir Robert Menzies

… and Melbourne humiliates Collingwood yet a-bloody-again

Laughter and cheering in the background as a door opens.

The noise is muffled as the door closes.

BARASSI *is carrying the 1964 premiership cup. He sits down with it. He turns the cup upside down and sits on it.*

Should I remind Melbourne supporters that if Melbourne hadn't broken discipline in 1958, if they'd all followed Norm Smith's orders; Melbourne would have won six premierships in a row? Imagine the Weg poster.

A mock-up of a Weg poster showing:
   'MELBOURNE WINS 55, 56, 57, 58, 59, 60 FLAGS'

Or would that be too cruel to mention?

The door opens again to the sounds of 'Three cheers to Froggy Crompton's lucky goal'. 'Hip hip hooray'.

BARASSI *gets off the cup, picks it up and puts it beside him on the bench.*

The door closes.

NORM *enters and sits down next to his foster son.*

BARASSI: I played like a dog.

NORM: You picked up in the last 15 minutes.

BARASSI: Nerves… couldn't shake my nerves—

NORM: Most agonising Grand Final I've experienced. Dicko is still weeping out there.

BARASSI: From sheer relief.

NORM: The best side didn't win today.

BARASSI: I know—without Froggy's lucky goal…

NORM: Crompton disobeyed my express orders…

BARASSI: We would have lost.

NORM: … to never go past centre half forward.

BARASSI: Froggy picked up a mark I spilled.

NORM: He shouldn't have been there.

BARASSI: Norm, he came out of nowhere, grabbed what I should never have spilled, and then kicked this perfect punt off one step.

NORM: It's like '58.

BARASSI: Oh God, Norm! Six years ago / give it a rest!

NORM: But Froggy brings it back—it still hurts inside, when you all promised me at halftime that you wouldn't go back out there and fight? And what the hell happened? In five minutes you were all punching the daylights out of Collingwood. No, Neil Crompton went against what I said and I don't give a damn if he kicked the winning goal. It's about the principle of the thing. Winning is important—it's damn important—but it's not as important as sticking to solid principles. If you deviate from principles, you deteriorate quickly.

The two men glance at each other. Pause.

It's Len's offer, isn't it?

BARASSI: No.

MELBA: Len Smith was resigning as coach of Richmond.

NORM: My brother had no bloody right...

BARASSI: You're barking / up the... [wrong tree]

NORM: ... to ask a Barassi to coach Richmond.

BARASSI: It's not Len's offer.

NORM: I told him you'd laugh at it.

BARASSI: I didn't laugh at it.

NORM: You should have.

BARASSI: I've not been given to laughter lately.

NORM: You've got the summer to rest, work on your business, spend time with the kids—with the *wife*.

BARASSI: I got *another* offer.

NORM: What offer?

BARASSI: 6,000 quid to coach.

NORM: 6,000 pounds?

BARASSI: Yes.

NORM: Well, if it's the money...

BARASSI: It's not the money—

NORM: Who is so bloody carefree that he doesn't care about 6,000 quid?

BARASSI: It's not *just* the money.

NORM: Who wants you?

BARASSI: Carlton.

NORM: Carlton!... Carlton? Ron Barassi coach of Carlton?!

BARASSI: Captain-coach—

NORM: Tell me that Martians have landed in Footscray, that men will never again go to war but don't tell me a Barassi is defecting to Carlton. Cripes! 6,000 pounds?

BARASSI: It's not just the money, Norm.

NORM: Then stay, stay at Melbourne.

BARASSI: I have these ideas.

NORM: Yeah, you're full of them.

BARASSI: We have to lift the game by lifting basic skills.

They talk over each other.

NORM: If a player can't kick a / football…

BARASSI: I see top players still making…

NORM: … by the time he /gets to senior level.

BARASSI: … fundamental mistakes. [*Pause.*] I'd take them all back to basics—raise the skill level.

NORM: Only a bad coach wastes time on that stuff.

BARASSI: You were the one that told me I'd be a good coach.

NORM: And one day you will be and you'll be a bloody good coach of Melbourne.

BARASSI: But when, when?

NORM: When I'm too bloody old.

BARASSI: I can't wait that long.

NORM: It won't be that long.

BARASSI: Nancy / thinks—

NORM: Nancy Barassi is devoted to Melbourne.

BARASSI: Nancy supports me.

NORM: Hard to understand.

BARASSI: What do you mean?

NORM *shakes his head but says nothing.*

She agrees that the money will go to the kids' education.

NORM: The best education for kids is to see loyalty in their parents.

BARASSI: The world is changing, Norm.

NORM: No, no, it's not—it's people who are changing.

Silence.

So your mind is made up?

BARASSI: I haven't slept for weeks over this.

NORM: Your dad gave his life for a decent world.

BARASSI: I want to do the decent thing. Christ, Norm—can't you see that?!

NORM: He was Melbourne and you're Melbourne and now we have Ron Barassi the third. What will you tell him about breaking his legacy?

BARASSI: I've nearly cried tears thinking about all this—like a bloody girl.

NORM: Stay here. Stay at Melbourne.

BARASSI: As what?

NORM: Captain. I know the hell of going to another club. I was never happy at Fitzroy. Never. And Carlton is as screwed up and back biting of a bastard bunch as Fitzroy was in '48. You'll be unhappy there. Melbourne is your home.

There is another big cheer offstage.

We should go back in.

BARASSI: On the 'Tony Charlton Football Show'—you know the award for Best Player?

NORM: What are you talking about?

BARASSI: You were on the panel, the Tony Charlton show, you gave me one vote, one vote out of a possible three votes on the best game I'd ever played, maybe in my life. One vote—everyone, not just me, but everyone said I played the best that day but because of you—the prize was given to someone else.

NORM: You wanted a silly TV show to give you a prize?

BARASSI: No, Norm, I didn't, I didn't want the prize. I wanted your vote, I just wanted your vote.

Pause.

NORM: I'll stand down.

BARASSI: As coach?

NORM: It's yours. The job is yours—we can't lose you.

BARASSI: You've just won Melbourne its sixth premiership in ten years.

NORM: Melbourne can't lose another Barassi.

BARASSI: It's your job, Norm.

NORM: Now it's yours.

BARASSI: I can't take your job if you're not ready to leave.

NORM: I'm as ready as I'll ever be.

BARASSI: You're the coach of Melbourne.

NORM: And you're its heartbeat.

>*Silence.*

BARASSI: You'd do this for me?

NORM: And for the club.

BARASSI: I don't know what to say.

NORM: Marj will be pleased. I'll see more of Peter.

BARASSI: You once said you'd coach until you died.

NORM: I'm Melbourne, Ron, and I'll do what is best for Melbourne and losing you from Melbourne will not be good for Melbourne.

>*He stands up and holds out his hand.*

Let's shake on it.

>BARASSI *stands. He's about to shake:*

BARASSI: But what will you do?

NORM: Perhaps I'll be chairman of selectors. I'll be your backup.

BARASSI: Like Checker Hughes was for you?

NORM: And like Percy Beames was for Checker.

BARASSI: When Checker Hughes had an opinion you didn't like, you sent him into the stands.

NORM: It would be different between you and me.

BARASSI: I don't know, Norm. I just…

NORM: Sleep on it.

BARASSI: Sleep?

NORM: You'll know when you know.

BARASSI: *I know* I want to see if I'm a good coach in my own right. That way if I succeed, it's mine and if I fail, it's my failure. *I know* that I want to be as good, if not better than you.

NORM: Big words.

BARASSI: *I also know* I don't want to force you out.

>*A tipsy player,* NEIL 'FROGGY' CROMPTON, *comes out.*

FROGGY: Hey! [*Indicating the premiership cup*] We want to fill that with champagne.

BARASSI: Froggy! I want to fill you with champagne, boy!

>FROGGY *takes the cup and does a little happy dance.*

>NORM *whispers to* BARASSI.

NORM: Tell me before you tell anyone, tell me your decision.

FROGGY: Come back to the party.

NORM: [*to* FROGGY] You shouldn't have been up there. What were you doing there?!

> NORM *exits and* FROGGY *is deflated.*

FROGGY: You think I did right, don't you, Captain?

BARASSI: It was the sweetest, truest, most glorious kick of the whole darn season.

FROGGY: My only goal of the whole darn season! First goal in five years— the boys reckon I did the right thing—I know I did the right thing.

BARASSI: Nothing feels better than knowing you did the right thing— you made your choice and you did your best under pressure.

FROGGY: Nothing in the whole wide world.

BARASSI: You're Melbourne's hero.

FROGGY: I'm just like Ron Barassi!

> FROGGY *picks up the cup.* BARASSI *pats him on the back as he leaves.*

> *As the door opens the other players yell out their congratulations again. The door closes.*

> *It's quiet.* BARASSI *stands there deep in thought. He walks slowly out the other way to the sounds of the 1965 hit 'Don't Let Me be Misunderstood' by The Animals.*

> *He takes off his Melbourne jumper and looks in the mirror. He sees the* OLDER BARASSI *staring back.*

> MELBA *hands them Carlton football jumpers. Together they put on the jumpers.*

> USHERS *come out selling Four 'N' Twenty pies.*

USHER 1: Get ya Four 'N' Twenty Pies!

USHER 2: Four 'N' Twenty Pie!

MELBA: Halftime, folks. Game re-commences in 20 minutes!

> *The* USHERS *go out into the auditorium and sell to the audience as they go into the foyer.*

END OF ACT ONE

ACT TWO

PROLOGUE

MELBA: 1960s Melbourne was a simpler place, a series of villages.

Melba walks through a flood of images of '60s Melbourne.

After Word War Two wave after wave of the war-affected would come across three oceans by boat to this big strange land. The often-bedraggled bunch, including me and Dad, learnt real quick that to get accepted, to have something to talk about with the locals, you need to choose a footy team. Within a few games a new excitement gripped us, all scarved and beanied up, we'd walk with our new mates to the home ground. Memories of soccer and rugby dimmed as a fresh passion filled our new life and this big, strange, lonely, far-off place became our home.

> MELBA *claps and the images stop at a huge newspaper headline:*
> *'CARLTON DRAFT*
> *MELBOURNE BITTER'*

SCENE ONE: THE DEATH OF LOYALTY

The OLDER BARASSI *walks on in a Carlton football jumper. He is being chased by a* JOURNALIST.

JOURNALIST: Ron, where's your heart?

BARASSI: [*pointing to his heart*] It's right here.

JOURNALIST: In football?

BARASSI: [*it's well-rehearsed*] I think your heart is where you are at, at the time. No matter who I play for I give everything for the guernsey, whether that be for Melbourne or Carlton or for Manangatang Thirds.

He walks off and the JOURNALIST *chases him.*

Four PEOPLE *walk on stage with their number 31 jumpers. One cuts it up with scissors, another jumps on it, the third sets it alight and the fourth pulls it apart with his bare hands.*

We hear a boy crying out in anger.

FATHER: [*offstage*] Simon, come back here!

SIMON: [*offstage*] I hate him, I hate him, I hate him!

A Melbourne football jumper with the number 31 flies through the air and lands on the floor.

SIMON'S FATHER *enters.*

FATHER: Simon!

He picks up the jumper that has had the number 31 cut into shreds. He picks up all the destroyed Melbourne jumpers and takes them off.

MELBA: Victoria was in a state of shock. It was like that Bob Dylan going electric. It was Petrov coming in from the cold and Harold Holt never coming out from the cold.

NANCY comes in with her knitting. She is knitting Carlton scarves.

Here's Nancy, the loyal 1960s housewife. Raising three of Barassi's children in the outer suburbs of Melbourne.

NANCY turns on the wireless.

MELBA conducts the ENSEMBLE MEMBERS who sing a 1960s radio advertisement.

RADIO ANNOUNCER: Go ahead, Henry from Moonee Ponds.

HENRY: Leaving your football club is like leaving your family to move into another family down the street. The Smith boy moving in with the Harris's—it's unthinkable. It's high treason.

RADIO ANNOUNCER: Now go ahead, Beryl from Lilydale.

BERYL: It took me months and months of painful labour to train my budgie to say 'C'mon, Ron'.

BUDGIE: C'mon, Ron!

BERYL: What am I to do now?

BUDGIE: C'mon, Ron! C'mon, Ron!

NANCY changes the station on her wireless.

ENSEMBLE MEMBERS make a white noise sound—'Sschcchh!'

NANCY stops when she hears music: 'Whatcha Gonna Do About It?' by The Small Faces.

MELBA sings along to the song from the wireless.

NANCY: [*calling out to the kids*] Susan, Ronny, Richard—come and try on your new jumpers! We want to show Dad when he gets home! [*To herself as she goes out to find the kids*] If he gets home.

> *On the other side of the stage* BARASSI *walks on in his Carlton football jumper.*

> *A Carlton supporter calls out:*

SUPPORTER: Are you going to pull your horns in now, Ronny?!

> BARASSI *pulls out a blackboard. On it, he writes the attributes needed to be a champion: 'LOYALTY' and 'COURAGE', then exits.*

> *Back at Heathmont the Eddie Miller hit song 'Please Release Me' is on the wireless.*

> MELBA *sings along with the song.*

NANCY: Susan, go find the boys!

> NANCY *rushes back in and, for a moment, looks at the wireless.*

> MELBA *is singing along.*

> NANCY *changes the station.*

> ENSEMBLE MEMBERS *make a white noise sound—'Sschccchh!'*

> NANCY *catches more talk radio.*

FEMALE CALLER: You know I always fancied that Ron Barassi—he's so handsome; like a movie star, I've got his picture beside my bed— but now? Now he's gone to Carlton I've completely turned off him.

NANCY: [*to the* CALLER] Good!

ELDERLY CALLER: I've been in tears about this all morning. If Barassi thinks he is too good for Melbourne, why has he gone to a lesser club?

> *As* NANCY *moves the dial,* ENSEMBLE MEMBERS *make the white noise sound—'Sschccchh!'—and exit.*

> NANCY *finds 'Please Release Me' again.*

> MELBA *is singing along.*

> NANCY *abruptly moves the dial again and catches more talk.*

RADIO ANNOUNCER: I'm speaking to George Harris, the president of Carlton, and a dentist in his spare time, and he is the man who has 'extracted'…

HARRIS: Very good, Lou.

RADIO ANNOUNCER: ... the man who has 'extracted' a 'yes' from former Melbourne champion Ron Barassi. So, George, is this the death of loyalty?

HARRIS: I told Ron. If you stay at Melbourne you will never be recognised as a teacher. We've all seen him on that TV show and he inspires the children of this country.

    NANCY *turns the wireless off.*

NANCY: Kids, c'mon. [*She holds up the Carlton jumpers.*] Look, just try them on.

    NANCY *exits as the Carlton* PLAYERS *come on in their work gear.*

SCENE TWO: OPENING SPEECH TO CARLTON

Carpenters, painters, students and office workers are changing into footy gear. As BARASSI *enters they all stop talking.*

BARASSI: Football is war and this is where you prepare yourself how to endure it. Gentlemen, this is not a training drill; it is a life and death battle—there are no practice matches—to get to the final—every match is a Grand Final—I am building a perfect team and to get a perfect team—practice doesn't make perfect! Only *perfect* practice makes perfect. At training, everything will be done at top pressure. If you can flatten a teammate and don't, you are letting him down, you are making him think football is easy—to ease off an opponent is to disrespect the opponent.

    He catches the eye of everyone in the room.

Those with wives and girlfriends, inform them under no circumstances are you to have sex the night before the game.

    He stares at everyone to see if they dare question this.

I want everyone to look at their diet. No big meat meals before the match, steak doesn't make you stronger, it just weighs you down. You will drink protein shakes and later on we will bring in an expert on diet and nutrition to consult with you on how to eat for maximum physical benefit.

    Someone pulls a face.

What was that, Wes? I demand total obedience, no laughs, no jokes, dress well and if you make a mistake you pay for it. If you are injured you wear red so I know not to push you too hard. If you're late you will wear yellow so I know to punish you. If you play badly on Saturday be prepared for a hell of a week ahead.

Silence.

Now there's been much talk about loyalty. I have an unusual slant on loyalty. I think loyalty is transportable.

PLAYER: [*whispering to another* PLAYER, *but is overheard*] I'll tell that to my wife if she ever hears about me mistress.

BARASSI: And all I want to hear from you when I talk to you is 'You're right, coach'. Well?

PLAYERS: [*together*] You're right, coach.

He looks at them all again. They all look steadily back at him.

BARASSI: Good, let's begin with eye work. One marker, three kickers.

They get into sequence.

Kicks occur in sequence up and down the line. Marker handballs back to the kicker.

The PLAYERS *begin training. They fumble and fall, some are nervous, others try so hard they make mistakes.*

Don't throw the ball. Punch it! Two hands, two bloody hands. Use strong hands, strong hands. Hold the bloody thing. One grab! It's just a state of mind. *Concentrate!* Kenny, mark with your eyes. Watch the ball come right into your hands, then look at it in there! No drop kicks, you drop kick! I don't care if it's your favourite kick. Drop kicks are not accurate. Now talk. Talk to each other. Gary. Stay alert! Football changes in an instant! From defence to attack from attack to defence and you've got to have a mind quick enough to grasp the difference the instant it happens and position yourself accordingly.

The PLAYERS *concentrate but are clearly nervous.*

Stephen! Pathetic! Were you bloody dreaming? Twenty laps for ignoring that call on your right. All of you, 20 penalty laps for Stephen.

The PLAYERS *run out.*

BARASSI *stops a player who is wearing number 31 on his back—*
GARY CRANE.

Gary, one minute. Look, mate, do you want a lower number? I know
a lot of players do.

They exchange jumpers as ELZA *walks into a butcher shop. There
is the tinkle of the butcher's bell as she walks in.*

BARASSI *has his hands on his back unconsciously caressing the
number 31.*

SCENE THREE: ELZA AT THE BUTCHERS

A BUTCHER *enters.*

ELZA: Could I pick up my order please? Five chops and a leg of lamb for
Brewster.
BUTCHER 1: [*to* BUTCHER 2, *out the back*] Order for Brewster!
BUTCHER 2: [*out the back*] Nothing here for Brewster!
BUTCHER 1: Sorry, love, nothing here for Brewster.
ELZA: I left my order. Oh, I know. Maybe I wrote Barassi. I still do that
sometimes, if I'm rushing.
BUTCHER 1: Barassi—like the football star?
BUTCHER 2: [*out the back*] We should have Barassi working here!
ELZA: Why?
BUTCHER 1: He can make lamb out of mutton, Mrs!
BUTCHER 2: [*out the back*] Didn't he give the Hawks a hiding
yesterday?
BUTCHER 1: If I was a Carlton player I'd be too scared to lose.
BUTCHER 2: [*out the back*] With that face he pulls—only a mother could
love!
ELZA: And I do.
BUTCHER 2: [*out the back*] Even she must have her doubts!
ELZA: [*loudly*] Ron Barassi is my son!

BUTCHER 2 *comes out from around the back with a dead pig in his
hand. He can't believe it.* BUTCHER 1 *dashes out the back and gets
her parcel.*

BUTCHER 1: Here's your chops and lamb, Mrs Barassi.

BUTCHER 2: You're Ron Barassi's mother?

ELZA: What were you expecting—a gorilla?

She leaves with her parcel.

SCNENE FOUR: TRAINING NIGHT, PRINCES PARK

BARASSI: [*like a gorilla*] For [*bleeped out*] sake! You useless wonder—
how can you *possibly* miss a handpass from that distance! Tell me
how you could miss that if you were really trying! Talk! Talk! Talk!
To each other! Is that the way you'd do it in a match, you mug? That
could cost us a *goal!*

He enters the auditorium and calls out to a row of seats.

If you want to be a top League footballer—you've got to be good at
every single aspect of the game. You know what you do well. Okay,
you're a good kick but your handpassing is weak so I want you to
work over and over until you are strong in every department.

He goes to another row.

Now you—yeah; you, look at me! You're too slow. Football is a
running game. I need my players to be fast. How do you get faster?
You jog and you sprint and you sprint. It's that simple.

He eyeballs another row.

Come here, come here—yeah you! You dropped three marks. That
would cost us a game! I want to make a point, so that you understand
something now and for all time! There are fellows who want to
succeed at everything they do. They want to win at *every single thing*
they tackle! They're *my* sort of guys! Now work on your marking,
okay?

To the room:

Now I'm going to notice your weakness and I'll notice if there is no
improvement over the weeks.

He eyeballs another row.

I'll be monitoring you—all of you—very closely. Like ASIO, I'll
know what you've done.

He thinks he hears someone moan.

Did I hear someone whinge like a girl? Winners never blame anybody. It's only losers who try to blame other people for what went wrong. So never con yourself that your failures and your weaknesses are someone else's fault.

He approaches a different row of seats.

Now you, yeah you. Yeah, I bark and I bloody bite too when I see someone slacking off. Now you're good, you're gifted. The failing of a lot of gifted people is that everything comes too easy for them. You know you're good because you've watched other players struggle with what you find a pushover. So you're overconfident. You don't drive yourself. A champion drives himself in everything he attempts. Remember: nobody's got any right to be proud of natural ability—that came to you through the eye of your father's [*beep*].

He gets back on stage and claps.

Okay. We're not breaking early because of the heat, but because you've done some good work tonight. Those of you who came down by car, run four more laps; the rest of you run back to the club. And I'll see you again when we face Melbourne.

Light comes up on the familiar figure of NORM SMITH *in his gabardine coat.*

He has the number 31 in his hand. A young player, RAY GROOM, *runs on and* NORM *hands him the number.* GROOM *takes off his guernsey with the number 15 and replaces it with No 31.*

MELBA: Melbourne easily beat Carlton in the first game against them. Norm Smith teaches his famous charge humiliation, little knowing that he was on the eve of the biggest humiliation of his life.

SLIDE: Headline 'NORM SMITH IS SACKED'

Meanwhile Carlton is on a losing streak. The Carlton boys are on the way to the pub to commiserate their loss. At Carlton they play hard but they party harder and Barassi doesn't like it. Especially when they are losing.

BARASSI *enters and sees them.*

SCENE FIVE: BARASSI BREAKS HIS TOE

BARASSI: Where are you all going?

PLAYER 3: Pub.

PLAYER 2: Need a drink, coach.

BARASSI: None of you deserves a drink! I've had a gutful of this sort of thing... *Mistakes!* ... *Not caring!* ... *Sloppiness!* ... I've had a *gutful* of it! You bloody sheilas—you were like a bunch of girls playing with Barbie dolls today. We lost against North Melbourne, NORTH MELBOURNE—the [*bleeped out*] wooden spooners! That pack of Ken dolls and you... I was ashamed.

PLAYER 3: So will you be going back to Melbourne now that they've given Norm the chop?

BARASSI: Norm Smith is the best coach the VFL has seen and I had to earn his respect and I did that by playing to the best of my ability. None of you earned my respect today!

PLAYER 1: But they kicked Norm out because he didn't want you to take his job.

BARASSI: That's bullshit!

PLAYER 2: It's in all the papers.

BARASSI *kicks the wall and breaks his toe.*

BARASSI: [*bleeped out*] [*bleeped out*] I've broken my bloody toe.

The PLAYERS *try not to laugh.*

Don't bloody laugh—we're out of the finals!

The PLAYERS *try even harder not to laugh.*

BARASSI *hops off.*

SCENE SIX: BARASSI AT HOME

SLIDE: Heathmont brick veneer, late 1960s

NANCY *hands* BARASSI *some crutches.*

BARASSI: Susan, Ronny! [*He sees them up a tree.*] Hey, get down from up there!

NANCY: They love it up there. How are you coping?

BARASSI: We are on this losing streak and...

NANCY: Why don't you talk to Norm?

BARASSI: I've got to convince the committee to buy me more players. There's this boy from Canberra.

NANCY: He'd love to give you some advice.

BARASSI: Melbourne will reinstate him.

NANCY: He's so knowledgeable, it would mean a lot to him at this time.

> BARASSI *shakes his head.*

I miss Norm and Marj and Melbourne, the social club. Living out here and not knowing the Carlton wives—it gets a bit… [lonesome]

> BARASSI *starts to hop away on his crutches.*

You're not going out again, are you?

BARASSI: Meeting Sir Robert Menzies tonight.

NANCY: What, in his Rolls?

BARASSI: Bentley. He may personally buy us some players.

NANCY: Will we have to vote for his party?

BARASSI: I need him. There is no fire in my forward flank.

NANCY: [*wryly*] Yeah, I've noticed.

> BARASSI *chooses to not respond to* NANCY*'s last sentence.*
>
> *The kids start fighting in the trees.*

BARASSI: Gotta go, love. Gotta convince this boy from Canberra—we gotta sign him before North Melbourne grabs him. See ya, kids!

SCENE SEVEN: ENTER ALEX JESAULENKO

Car advertisement music.

MELBA: Enter Alex Jesaulenko.

ENSEMBLE 1 & 2: [*together*] Oh, Jesaulenko, you beauty!

> *A fit-looking tall player poses in a Carlton jumper, as if he is on a catwalk.*

MELBA: Canberra-raised, Salzburg-born, from Ukrainian refugee parents. Feline agility—superb high marking, the rare combination of perfect balance and prodigious goal-kicking. In 1970 this Ukrainian gazelle was clocked kicking six goals in 11 minutes. But Alex did more than kick a bag of goals—he changed us. He made us better people. You see, when Jezza took that mark of the century in the 1970 Grand Final, Australia realised 'Wogs are okay!'

The dance of Jezza. He climbs up the back of a man and marks as if he is a ballet dancer.

The advertisement is interrupted by:

SCENE EIGHT: WALLS IN A WALL

BARASSI *is slamming a* PLAYER *into a wall.*

BARASSI: I saw you kick that player. That was a dirty act.

BARASSI *slams him again.*

I don't ever want to see you do the dirty thing again. You do the right thing. Okay?

PLAYER: Right, coach.

BARASSI: Look at me.

The PLAYER *looks at him.*

You look someone in the eye when they talk to you, you shake hands firmly, treat people with respect and admit when you make a mistake.

PLAYER: You're right, coach.

BARASSI *holds his hand out to shake. The* PLAYER *is about to shake it when* BARASSI *shakes the passing* JESAULENKO. JESAULENKO *and* BARASSI *laugh like drains while the* PLAYER *looks unamused. Then* BARASSI *does a real handshake with the* PLAYER *and pats his back.*

BARASSI: [*good naturedly*] You right to come to Heathmont tonight? Bring the girlfriend, Nancy is cooking. I'll pick you up from Brunswick.

PLAYER: With Doug?

BARASSI: Yeah, we'll pick Dougie up as well.

MELBA: Barassi drove his players all over Melbourne getting more speeding fines than was good for him. He drove his Merc like he drove his players, hard, fast and with impatient pleasure.

SLIDE: Headline 'BARASSI DROPPED FROM CARLTON'

Barassi has to stop playing—he has to face it: he's only getting a game because he's living with the coach. From the sidelines he can concentrate—

The lights change to a stadium.

The sounds of a crowd.

SCENE NINE: CARLTON PLAY RICHMOND AND LOSE

MELBA: Carlton plays Richmond in the finals.

The sounds of a crowd excited—a goal is kicked.

BARASSI *is in a late 1960s suit. He is high in the stand talking into his phone. He shakes his head in deep frustration. He paces, jumps, paces, gesticulates, and at one stage goes onto his knees.*

BARASSI: [*into the phone*] You dickhead, I have been yelling at you to swap, swap with Walls.

He's watching and the tension in his body is palpable.

The crowd cheer out encouragement.

BARASSI *jumps and stomps down hard as the ball misses a goal.*

Where were you, Jezza? [*Into the phone*] Tell Jezza to stay in front of his man.

The crowd are quieter now.

BARASSI *is watching intensely.*

Give it to him! Give it to him! Oh, Christ! Why did you give it to him? If you're going to make a mistake, make it a bloody good one. Pathetic! [*Into the phone*] Tell if he doesn't bloody handball, I'll handball him up the [*bleeped out*]! [*Listening to the phone*] What?! [*Looking out*] Why is he going there? [*Into the phone*] Tell him I want obedient players, yes, but not bloody sheep!

NANCY *enters.*

[*Looking out*] Go for it! Don't' be a nancy, [*bleeped out*] nancy boy. Ah, pathetic!

NANCY: Ron!

BARASSI: The Tigers are winning, Nancy.

NANCY: Your players are scared of you!

BARASSI: I want them to be scared of me. I want them to be too bloody scared to lose.

NANCY: The children are tired. I want to take them home. I don't know anyone here.

The crowd are stirred up and BARASSI *sees a goal kicked by Richmond.*

BARASSI: No, no, no, *NO!*

The siren sounds and BARASSI *bashes the phone against the wall. He holds his head in his hands and sways. An* OFFICIAL *goes to talk to* BARASSI *but* NANCY *stops him.*

NANCY: He just wants to be alone for a moment. He has put a lot into the day and now it's over.

She leads the OFFICIAL *out.*

BARASSI *comes back down from the stand.*

BARASSI: I need someone, a weapon—someone who can go anywhere that's weak—an interchange—a fearless tiger.

SCENE TEN: ENTER BRENT CROSSWELL

1960s car advertisement music.

MELBA: 1968. Enter Brent Crosswell.

A serious-looking, fit and strong BRENT CROSSWELL *enters.*

Wild and untamed. Chess-playing and left-wing. Crosswell was a highly skilled and flamboyant player.

CROSSWELL: Give me a grey day at the Western Oval and 15,000 people and I wasn't worth a cracker; give me 90,000 people at the MCG and I am Hercules.

MELBA: Given a Barassi spray he would mumble poetry to himself.

CROSSWELL: To offend and judge are distinct offices, and of opposed natures.

MELBA: Crosswell wanted to fit in; which was difficult. As that young newspaper fella, Martin Flanagan wrote: 'He was an intellectual and a footballer at a time when you weren't allowed to be both'. He needs one more weapon in his arsenal.

SCENE ELEVEN: ENTER SYD JACKSON

1960s car advertisement music.

MELBA: Enter Syd Jackson—Syd, a child of the Stolen Generation, is a gifted, courageous Aboriginal footballer, brilliantly skilful both sides of his body, the first person to introduce the banana kick into Australian footy.

    JACKSON *banana kicks.*

More than any other player, Barassi's style of football, that demands fewer kicks, more handballing and more goals, suited young Jackson. He would become Carlton's greatest goal sneak.

SCENE TWELVE: THE CONGA LINES OF 1968 AND 1969

Conga music.

SLIDE: *Headline 'THE BATTLING BLUES WIN BY THREE POINTS'*

MELBA: 1968. The Blues take home the flag. Carlton hadn't won a premiership for 21 years.

    A line of conga dancers celebrate the Grand Final win. The Carlton PLAYERS, *led by* BARASSI, *are delirious with happiness.*

ENSEMBLE: [*together*] Barassi! Barassi! Barassi!

    They conga offstage.

MELBA: 1969.

    Another line of conga dancers wearing Richmond jumpers conga back in.

ENSEMBLE: [*together*] Hafey! Hafey! Hafey!

    A dejected BARASSI *is interviewed by a journalist.*

JOURNALIST: How do you feel about Carlton just missing out on the '69 Grand Final?

BARASSI: My top players were all playing badly that day but in 1970 I predict that Carlton will again win the Grand Final.

    Carly Simon sings 'You're So Vain'—during which the Carlton PLAYERS *train hard.*

SCENE THIRTEEN: 1970

A training session is in progress. This training session is more slick. The Carlton PLAYERS *all dance with the ball. They have elegance, fitness and style.*

BARASSI *walks amongst them.*

BARASSI: Whenever you get tired think of Captain Cook—*The Endeavour, The Endeavour!* Hey, Syd, don't slow down—always remember Captain Cook.

JACKSON: How can I forget him, coach? He's the bloke that took all our land.

> JACKSON *does a few steps of a traditional Aboriginal dance and finishes with his iconic banana kick.* BARASSI *is impressed.*

MELBA: It's a new decade. Bodies are hardened, discipline sharpened and destinies written. Carlton makes the Grand Final against the Mighty Pies.

> *The now familiar roar of the crowd.*

> *SLIDE: Image of the Melbourne Cricket Ground, 1970*

It's the end of the first quarter and we are thrashing the living suitcases out of Carlton!

COMMENTATOR: Collingwood 4.8.32 to Carlton 0.3.3 in the first quarter.

MELBA: Let's take a peek inside the Carlton clubrooms, shall we?

> *She clicks her fingers and we instantly see inside the Carlton clubrooms.* PLAYERS *are sheepishly gathering.*

Collingwood is playing like a sleek, clean machine and Barassi is filthy.

> BARASSI *enters, wearing a tight '70s suit with big collar.*

BARASSI: I am not going to take the rap for this performance. Everybody out! That includes you, Mr Menzies sir. Only the players to stay, thank you.

> *He storms around the room, eyeballing everyone.*

There was only a lousy stinking rotten 20 handballs. I don't see anyone playing like footballers today except for Crosswell and he can't be our only bloody player! Goold, you replace Pinnell on the wing. Crane, you go to centre and Walls to the wing. McKay, you go to the ruck. Now dodge those big blokes and, if you can't dodge them, handball over them. I want you boys to go all out now! I want risks, bloody risks, if you're going to make a mistake make it a big one! I need you to be bold, be bold. If it is possible to create a nine-goal turnaround in three quarters, why can't an eight goal turnaround be achieved in two quarters. We have not lost this! We will not lose this!

A siren—the PLAYERS *run out.*

MELBA: At the end of second quarter Collingwood is seven goals three points ahead. I crack a bottle of champers.

> MELBA *has cranked the scoreboard:*
> *Collingwood 10.13.73, Carlton 4. 5.29*

Look at how we scored! Blues supporter should line up and demand a refund on their ticket! The Pies are home, hosed and munching on a Chiko roll! Take a look at the opposition, shall we?

> MELBA *clicks her finger.*

> *SLIDE: Image of the MCG change rooms*

> *Carlton* PLAYERS *creep back in, drink cordial and place ice on injuries, et cetera.* MELBA *walks among them. She picks up the chin of a dejected face and lets it flop down again.*

> BARASSI *opens the door and the noise of the crowd enters the room. He stands there for a moment with the familiar scowl on his face. All the* PLAYERS *are completely still.* BARASSI *walks inside and the door closes behind him. The crowd noise disappears and the* PLAYERS *all nervously look to their coach.*

BARASSI: We are 44 points behind.

> *The silence is thick.*

But Collingwood is tiring.

> *The* PLAYERS *can't believe how gentle he has become. He smiles— it looks all wrong on him.*

I want you all to know. Whether you win or lose from here. I'm proud of your efforts.

> *There is a stunned silence.* BARASSI *remains pleasant-faced.*

PLAYER 1: [*whispering to another* PLAYER] Has he lost his marbles?

PLAYER 2: Are you alright, Barass?

PLAYER 3: Coach, you okay?

PLAYER 1: Lose? Did he say it was okay to lose?

MELBA: Time, coach.

BARASSI: Get ready, Teddy—you're on.

> TEDDY HOPKINS, *man with a blonde mop of hair, jumps off the bench. And in his enthusiasm he trips over his undone shoelaces.*

HOPKINS: God. Me?

BARASSI: You're replacing Thornley.

HOPKINS: Ah, yes. God, yes, God. Yes!

> *Siren.*

> *The* PLAYERS *(except* HOPKINS *who is double-checking his laces) are still immobilised.*

CROSSWELL: Have you got anything more to say to us, coach?

BARASSI: Yes. HANDBALL, HANDBALL, HANDBALL!

> *The three words reverberate around the theatre.*

> *The* PLAYERS *run out.*

> *Two simultaneous broadcasts go out—the first commentary is reflective, the second is a live commentary of the last few moments of the game.*

> *Lights on* MELBA *and* BARASSI *as they watch the game.*

DOCUMENTARY VOICE-OVER: [*an old-fashioned radio-style voice*] Ted Hopkins had been give a small role in the 1970 Grand Final—he ended up taking the lead in front of a record crowd of 121,000 people in one of the greatest comebacks in VFL history. Hopkins had been on the bench most of the year but after halftime he kicked four magnificent goals to carve his name into the game's history and was hardly heard of again.

COMMENTATOR 1: There's nobody there!

COMMENTATOR 2: LOOK AT THIS!

COMMENTATOR 1: It's bounced through!

COMMENTATOR 3: You wouldn't believe this, honestly. That's Jesaulenko's third goal.

COMMENTATOR 2: Hopkins kicked four, Crosswell two, Jackson one.

COMMENTATOR 3: And Collingwood players holding hands to their heads as the time's getting away from them now.

COMMENTATOR 1: You wouldn't see anything better anywhere in the world, Butch, as far as excitements and highlights and tremendous sportsmen are concerned.

COMMENTATOR 3: Ricky Mott with the ball in the centre of the ground.

COMMENTATOR 2: Is there time? McKenna comes out. Hall punches away. A grand finish by Hall, ah, they're, they're just too disciplined, the kick going up to the flank and O'Callaghan drops the mark, he plays on again, shorts one into the centre, plays on, Price has it, he's in trouble. Right across the centre, still looking desperately for McKenna. A chance for Twiggy Dunn!

A surge from the crowd.

COMMENTATOR 1: Ah, beautiful mark!

MELBA: Go, Twiggy!

COMMENTATOR 3: Oh, what a great finish, boy, these fellas have got hearts as big as themselves!

COMMENTATOR 2: You can say that again!

MELBA: Go, Twiggy! Go, Twiggy! Go, Twiggy!

COMMENTATOR 1: Twenty-eight and a half minutes gone in the final quarter of the 1970 Grand Final.

COMMENTATOR 2: Carlton have come from a mile behind, no other way to describe it.

COMMENTATOR 1: And you wouldn't want to have a crook heart, would you?

COMMENTATOR 3: Twiggy Dunn has kicked two goals and he would be 40 yards out directly in front.

MELBA: God bless you to kick it straight, kick it true, young man.

COMMENTATOR 3: He kicks, oh…

The crowd squeals in dismay.

MELBA: Ooooh!

COMMENTATOR 3: … it's swinging off, and it's—ooh!—one point, one point!

MELBA: No, no, noooo!

COMMENTATOR 1: It's all over for the Magpies again, Mike, there's no worries in the world about that now, they just haven't got the time.

COMMENTATOR 2: Look, Barassi is still looking desperately worried about this and I wouldn't be worried if I was him.

COMMENTATOR 3: Now to Crane, his kick up towards the half forward flank, Adamson and Jackson—

COMMENTATOR 2: Jackson races for it, Adamson beats him to it this time, Jackson pulls him to the ground and the ball goes over for a throw-in.

COMMENTATOR 3 Free kick going to Adamson. Sorry, Adamson's free.

Siren.

BARASSI *shoots up into the air and* MELBA *falls to the ground.*

Black.

Through the black the scoreboard shines through:
   Collingwood 14.17. 101, Carlton 17. 9. 111

MELBA *is beside the scoreboard. For a moment she is silent.*

MELBA: For Collingwood fans the feeling of loss that day was akin to the breakup of a marriage. How could it happen when we were so good together, we had so much love, so much belief—how could we have lost? How did it die?

ENSEMBLE 3: How do you know you're a Collingwood supporter?

ENSEMBLE 2: When the person you admire the most is Jack Daniels?

MELBA *gives the boys the hairy eyeball before she begins to sing the Whitlam political campaign jingle 'It's Time'.*

SLIDE: An image of a youthful Gough Whitlam

The Carlton PLAYERS *all join in the song.*

SLIDES:Images of anti-Vietnam War protesters, Germaine Greer, et cetera

The Carlton PLAYERS *are passing around a joint as they sing.*

BARASSI *walks in and the music stops. The* PLAYERS *try to hide what they are smoking and try not to giggle.* BARASSI *takes a big breath, then smiles.*

BARASSI: Alright, boys—I've gathered you here to tell me what's on your mind. We are losing matches and I want to know why. Let's get everything out in the open.

CROSSWELL: This talk is without prejudice?

SYD JACKSON *giggles.* BARASSI *glares then tries to smile again.*

BARASSI: Yes, I want this talk to be free and honest. Does anyone want to start? Jones. You look like a man with something on his mind.

Silence.

I want to hear what you have to say. [*Pause.*] Percy?

JONES: Getting pilloried by you is giving me my worst season, coach.

Silence.

BARASSI: Okay, now Brent.

CROSSWELL: When winning is everything and losing is not just losing but failing—you make us feel ashamed—if winning is all that matters, what are the implications of that philosophy for a civilised community?

A couple of the boys giggle at that.

BARASSI: Rob?

WALLS: I didn't invite you to my 21st because I'm jack of you, man.

BARASSI: And Syd?

JACKSON: You're the only coach I want coaching me, Barass. But I'm not lazy, I haven't got a swollen head. I hate hearing this from you, coach. You know one day, just one day, I'd like you to come up to me with a smile on your face.

CROSSWELL: You plant the seeds carefully and then stomp us into the ground.

BARASSI *tries to keep calm but it's difficult.*

WALLS: And the no sex before the match rule…

All the men murmur in agreement, then begin giggling.

BARASSI: I've had a gutful of this.

BARASSI *turns to exit.*

CROSSWELL: You asked for our individual opinions.

BARASSI: In football individuals don't count. It isn't a game of bloody tennis or golf.

He looks at the PLAYERS. *Some suppress giggles others look stony-faced.*

Look at ya. Look at you all looking at me like I'm the bloody moron.

The PLAYERS *all try hard to stifle their giggles.*

I'm leaving. I'm going to make a big success out of office furniture.

The PLAYERS *burst into laughter.*

You know something. I'm going to say something I never thought I'd ever say but it's the truth. [*Pause.*] I'm sick of football.

Siren.

Black.

SCENE FIFTEEN: WHEELS ON CHAIRS

A spotlight on NORM SMITH *in a dinner suit.*

NORM: Nothing was impossible for Ron—that was what made the difference between him and everyone else. It was not the ability—it was the beat in the left breast. No player ever pulled on a Melbourne guernsey and gave more on more occasions than Ron. There was a cold fury burning in Barassi—he's never been beaten, it's just that the game was called off before he could win. He's made his father proud. [*He holds up a glass.*] To Ron. May we wish him well in his life beyond football.

There is a big cheer from the room.

Lights reveal BARASSI *putting on a suit jacket.* NANCY, *in dressing-gown, hands him his briefcase and sandwiches. She kisses him on the cheek. He stands there for a moment.*

A WORKER *walks over, taking his briefcase and sandwiches, and handing him a lease.*

WORKER 1: I'll need your signature.

BARASSI: I'll look at this later.

Another WORKER *comes in wheeling a '70s office chair.*

WORKER 2: This is the Supporto office chair.

He takes the contract out of BARASSI's *hand and gives it to* WORKER 1. *He pushes* BARASSI *in the chair and wheels him around flamboyantly.* WORKER 1 *follows.*

WORKER 1: Designed ergonomically.

BARASSI: Ergo what?

WORKER 1: Good for your back. They have adjustable seat heights.

WORKER 2 adjusts his seat height and wheels BARASSI *to his desk.*

BARASSI: Oh, right.

WORKER 1: And wheels.

BARASSI: Yes, wheels.

WORKER 1: Yes, so you can wheel around the office without getting out of your chair.

BARASSI: That's encouraging laziness, isn't it? God, you've been sitting on your arse all day in a chair—you should get out and walk to the bloody filing cabinet.

WORKER 1: It's the future.

Another WORKER *(*SALLY*) comes in with banking forms.*

WORKER 4: Sorry I'm late, the trains /… [were delayed]

BARASSI: Twenty push-ups now!

WORKER 4: Sir?

BARASSI: All of you, 20 penalty push-ups because of Sally.

They are about to do it.

I'm joking.

WORKER 2: I need you to sign the banking forms.

Placing the forms on his desk:

WORKER 3: And that lease signed.

Placing the lease on his desk:

WORKER 1: And the contract signed.

Placing the contract on his desk:

BARASSI: Righto.

The WORKERS *all look at him. He looks at the pile of paperwork.*

I'll get on to all of this right away.

WORKER 2: Okay, boss.

WORKER 3: Okay, boss.

WORKER 1: Okay, boss.

WORKER 4: Okay, sir.

They leave him.

He plays with his office chair.

BARASSI: Wheels. Wheels on bloody office chairs?

He shakes his head. He looks at the paperwork. He spins in his chair. He looks out of the window and sighs.

A football goes flying through the air. He holds up one arm and expertly grabs it.

ALBERT MANTELLO *enters.*

MANTELLO: Mr Barassi.

BARASSI: Mr Mantello—what can I do for you?

MANTELLO: I'm looking for a second-hand desk.

BARASSI: We don't sell second-hand desks.

MANTELLO *kicks the desk.*

MANTELLO: It's second-hand now.

BARASSI *smiles—he's on to* MANTELLO.

BARASSI: How are the Shinboners?

MANTELLO: We may be in the gutter but we are looking at the stars. North Melbourne is the proudest club in the League.

BARASSI: With the emptiest trophy cabinet.

MANTELLO: Can you imagine the day the Shinboners win their first ever Grand Final?

BARASSI: Would shut down the whole city.

MANTELLO: Can you imagine the satisfaction a coach would get from causing the city of Melbourne to shut down?

BARASSI: I sell office furniture. Look at this—wheels on office chairs.

MANTELLO: How do you feel about Nicholls coaching Carlton to win the premiership?

BARASSI: No need to get off your arse to walk to the filing cabinet.

MANTELLO: Barassi did all the hard work—Nicholls gets the glory.

BARASSI: [*patting the chair*] Satisfying stuff.

MANTELLO: You know we voted against introducing the 10-year rule.

BARASSI: If players give 10 years to a club they deserve their freedom.

MANTELLO: It's upset a lot of clubs.

BARASSI: Who wants to lose their best players?

MANTELLO: Yes, so while the other clubs are still griping, we'll go a-groping.

BARASSI: Who would you approach?

MANTELLO: You tell me.

BARASSI: I'd go for gold—Doug Wade, John Rantall and a Bomber—Davis, Barry Davis.

MANTELLO: Three captains.

BARASSI: They've all done their 10 years.

MANTELLO: And what else would you need?

BARASSI: Money.

MANTELLO: Naturally.

BARASSI: $50,000 cash injection for this business.

MANTELLO: Crikey.

BARASSI: Wheels aren't cheap.

MANTELLO: Fifth-thousand?

BARASSI: That I'd pay back at five per cent to start with.

MANTELLO: Keep talking.

BARASSI: And Norm Smith on the selection committee.

MANTELLO: Let's get this in writing, shall we?

> MANTELLO *pulls out a paper serviette.*

BARASSI: We are an office supply business, you realise?

MANTELLO: I like this better.

> MANTELLO *begins scribbling.*

BARASSI: With Norm Smith on my side, we can make miracles in this world.

MANTELLO: Sign here.

> BARASSI *signs.*

MELBA: Norm Smith died of a brain tumour a few months after Barassi moved to North Melbourne. He was 57 years old. Barassi had lost his football father.

SCENE SIXTEEN: BARASSI SPRAY

SLIDE: Arden Street Oval, 1973

There is the noise of the crowd.

It's halftime and BARASSI *is addressing his* PLAYERS. *He's in the centre and the* PLAYERS *make nervous circles around him.*

BARASSI: That's bloody right! Daryl. You are a [*bleeped out*]! I'll tell you why. You've got the bloody football game beaten. You've come down here and you haven't concentrated. The ball goes out towards the Carlton small men. You've stayed back with your man. You could've got to the Carlton small man but 'Oh no, I'm gonna protect myself'. I don't mind a bloke goin' bad, Daryl, but to me it's probably because you're bloody not switched on properly. Now you get over and try and mind the bloody forward pocket, okay? Stephen, you go to centre half back. And you go to full back. Now if you blokes think I'm bloody stirred up, you're bloody right. You're bloody right. If you are bloody fierce in your desire to do it right, you do it. Now I'm not gonna have the bloody forward line do well and the bloody backline play shithouse. This is too big a match and too much bloody at stake to bloody be like that.

NORM SMITH *hovers to the side in his gabardine coat.*

That bloody forward line's playing tremendous. Kevin Bryant Fantastic.

Siren.

The North Melbourne PLAYERS *run back onto the ground.*

BARASSI *stares at* NORM. *Just behind him is* SENIOR *in his Melbourne Football Club outfit.*

MELBA: Now you're probably thinking (and if you're not then you're bloody not switched on properly) that this is a story of Football, Fathers, Melbourne and War—and you're bloody right, you're bloody well right.

SCENE SEVENTEEN: THINGS FALL APART

SLIDE: Windy Hill football ground

MELBA: Barassi loved his players. And the players who gave their all, he'd take a bullet for.

Siren—the PLAYERS *run back on.*

> BARASSI *walks up to Essendon's captain-coach* DES TUDDENHAM *and screams at him.*

BARASSI: Tuddy. You leave off my Burns. You dirty bastard. You leave him off.

TUDDENHAM: Fuck off, Barassi.

BARASSI: If you go near my Burns again I'll bloody strangle you.

TUDDENHAM: Why wait?

> BARASSI *goes to strangle him. And* TUDDENHAM *fights back. Soon several North Melbourne* PLAYERS *are pulling the men apart.*

MELBA: Barassi in his fervour to raise the Kangaroos from the dead had dropped the ball on his furniture business.

> *The* PLAYERS *eventually pull the two warring men apart. They take* TUDDENHAM *away;* BARASSI *is left on his own.*
>
> *The crowd calls out: 'BARASSI! BARASSI! BARASSI!'*
>
> *He is handed a cup.*
>
> *The sounds of heartfelt applause.*

Around the same time, he lost the love and respect of a woman he vowed to God in his church to honour and cherish forever.

> NANCY *enters with a suitcase and drops it down beside him. She stands there and doesn't look at him.* BARASSI *takes his keys out, takes off the house key and hands it to her.* NANCY *takes the key without looking at him and walks away.*
>
> WORKER 1 *scoops him and his case up in his office chair. Men in suits are taking everything around him. They take Barassi's office chair, his desk, et cetera.*
>
> *The stage is left bare.* BARASSI *is left alone with the premiership cup. His three* WORKERS *walk on. They are sad.* BARASSI *hands each an envelope.*

WORKER 3: Bye, boss.

WORKER 2: Bye, boss.

WORKER 1: Bye, boss.

> WORKER 1 *goes to shake his hand.* BARASSI *holds out his hand but* WORKER 1 *goes past him and shakes the hand of* WORKER 3.

BARASSI *tries to laugh at the missing handshake gag that he had taught them. The three* WORKERS *give him a group hug and then leave taking the cup.*

BARASSI *stands alone.*

SCENE EIGHTEEN: BEST AND WORST OF TIMES

MELBA: 1975 was the worst of times.

> *SLIDE:* The Age *headline: 'GOUGH WHITLAM IS SACKED'*

And it was the best of times.

> *Music: Janice Joplin's 'Piece of My Heart'.*

Enter Cherryl with two r's. Artistic, Bohemian, part-Jewish, part-Aboriginal. And fully Original.

> CHERRYL *enters wearing an Afghan coat and a long blonde hair wig. With big '70s sunglasses.*

Barassi had never met a woman quite like her. When asked what she does with her life, Cherryl answers…

CHERRYL: I'm having a wonderful time.

> *She dances to the Joplin song.*

> BARASSI *approaches her.*

What side was it again that you play for?

> BARASSI *laughs a deep, happy laugh. She pulls him in close. There is a strong sexual attraction.*

BARASSI: Whitlam! / Whitlam was…

CHERRYL: Whitlam was exactly what this country needed.

BARASSI: The governor-general / had—

CHERRYL: The governor-general had no bloody right.

BARASSI: He / —

CHERRYL: Ron, I think if you read a bit more on the subject, you wouldn't make such an ignorant comment.

BARASSI: Gough Whitlam was—

> CHERRYL *stops him with a kiss.*

CHERRYL: You want to debate or do you want to learn?

They kiss again. It's sexy.

MELBA: 1981, and Cherryl and Barassi are married—the same year he returns to his first home, the now beleaguered Melbourne Football Club.

SLIDE: Headline 'THE PRODIGAL SON. HE'S BACK!'

SCENE NINETEEN: PRODIGAL SON

MELBA: It was the biggest news in the football world. Ron Barassi's return to Melbourne as a coach.

COMMENTATOR: Everyone has waited to see Ron Barassi back at Melbourne wearing his old and famous number 31. Every team the Super Coach has trained has been at the bottom of the ladder or near the bottom of the ladder and he has led them to seven Grand Finals.

MELBA: His return was front page news. His arrival was heralded as biblical. Jesus raising Lazarus from the dead.

A banner is brought on and put up at the back of the room. It reads: 'JUST HOW LONG DO WE WAIT BEFORE BECOMING WINNERS?'

NORM SMITH *stands ghostly beside the banner.*

COMMENTATOR: Barassi will be a success at Melbourne because he's Barassi: strong, dynamic, innovative, astute, thorough…

MELBA: Melbourne had been down and out ever since the Norm Smith era—they had not made the finals for 16 seasons in a row. It was called 'The Curse of Norm Smith'. The curse of ingratitude. But what Barassi found was a club with a severe skill shortage, and a new generation of players with a different upbringing—these young men were less willing to accept the hardline Barassi way.

MARK 'WHACKO' JACKSON *comes on in a Melbourne football jumper. He sings the two opening lines of his hit song 'I'm an Individual'.*

A chorus of other Melbourne PLAYERS *follow him in his dance routine. They sing the chorus.*

First game in with the new coach, Melbourne won by one point.

SLIDE: Headline 'BARASSI SWOOPS'

SLIDE: Headline 'THAT'S IT DEMONS, BARASSI IS BACK IN TOWN'

SLIDE: Headline 'BARASSI: MY TEAM TO WIN THE FLAG'

But it was a false dawn. The club had one outstanding player in wingman Robbie Flower, a handful of just okay players and a large percentage who just weren't up to VFL standard. In the first year Melbourne did not win another match and they slipped from second last on the ladder to unchallenged wooden spooners. The headlines from this time tell of hope and dreams crushed.

MELBA *puts on revolving headlines that slide across the stage.*

SLIDE: Headline 'BARASSI HITS OUT AT PROPHETS OF DOOM'

SLIDE: Headline 'BARASSI TANS DEMONS HIDE'

SLIDE: Headline 'BARASSI SWOOPS'

SLIDE: Headline 'THAT'S IT DEMONS, BARASSI IS BACK IN TOWN'

SLIDE: Headline 'BARASSI: MY TEAM TO WIN THE FLAG'

SLIDE: Headline 'WRONG MOVE RON!'

SLIDE: Headline 'DEMONS ROASTED ALL ROUND'

SLIDE: Headline 'BARASSI'S WORST YEAR'

SLIDE: Headline 'APPALLED, ASHAMED SAYS BARASSI'

SLIDE: Headline 'BARASSI FAILURE WINS 13 LOSSES 41'

Lights up on CHERRYL *drawing.*

Music: Stravinsky's 'Tango For Piano'.

SCENE TWENTY: THE KITTEN

BARASSI *comes home. He takes his muddy boots off and his wet coat. He's tired. The fire in the belly seems to have gone.*

The phone rings. BARASSI *looks to* CHERRYL *to answer it but she's fully absorbed. He lets the phone ring out.*

BARASSI *walks over and stares at* CHERRYL*'s work.*

CHERRYL: On my break while I was dusting the stove.
BARASSI: We must cook something in our kitchen one day.
CHERRYL: I heard this meowing outside the kitchen window.
BARASSI: Another one dumped?
CHERRYL: [*indicating a box*] Quite a character this one.

BARASSI *walks to the box.*

BARASSI: Hey, little fella.

The kitten purrs loudly.

[*Stroking the kitten*] Let's call him Koda.

CHERRYL: Coda—that's perfect—the final dance in a ballet.

BARASSI: I was thinking Koda—like short for Kokoda Trail.

She returns to her sketching.

The phone rings.

Can you get that?

CHERRYL: No, darling, absorbed in my higher self.

BARASSI *puts the kitten down and approaches the phone and stops and stares into the distance.*

SCENE TWENTY-ONE: GHOST OF NORM SMITH

MELBA: Now, Barassi is not a suspicious man. He doesn't believe in ghosts, fairies or Santa Claus. He knows Elvis Presley did indeed die on his bathroom floor in Finals week of '77. But right now this reasonable man could believe in curses.

Lights up slowly on where BARASSI *is staring. It's a ghostly outline of* NORM SMITH *in his iconic gabardine coat.*

The phone stops ringing.

NORM *stares at him with a look of sadness.*

CHERRYL *enters.*

CHERRYL: Who was on the phone?

BARASSI: No-one.

CHERRYL: You look ashen.

BARASSI: I've hired a psychologist to work on my players—maybe he should work on me?

CHERRYL: [*suggestively*] I know what needs working on.

BARASSI: Oh, yeah?

CHERRYL: Come with me.

BARASSI: Always.

CHERRYL *leads* BARASSI *out.*

A light stays on NORM. MELBA *and the* ENSEMBLE MEMBERS *gather around him.*

ENSEMBLE 1: Do you think he has cursed the Melbourne Football Club?

MELBA: No. I think he'd say that the Demons should remember where they came from and play like the noblest football club in Australia's history.

NORM smiles as his light begins to fade.

Norm.

The light on NORM *brightens for a moment.*

Before you go. Let me tell you a story about young Ronny. 44 years after your sacking, your foster son saw a man hit a woman and he chased that woman's attacker down the street. The values instilled in him by you and Elza, and by the noble game itself, guided him. Football—the football you coached, taught him selflessness and courage. Barassi showed the world that heroism can exist outside the football field.

ENSEMBLE 2: And he discovered another hero, Jimmy Stynes, who gave Melbourne back its heartbeat.

MELBA: Is it time, Norm?

ENSEMBLE 2: Could you lift the curse?

NORM gives ENSEMBLE 2 *a wink before his light fades completely out.*

SCENE TWENTY-TWO: THE COLD CALL

BARASSI *comes back in with a smile on his face and dishevelled hair. He skips to the phone and answers it.*

BARASSI: Yeah, hello.

How'd you get this number?

What? Security doors, no thanks, mate.

Is that all you're going to say? 'Sorry to bother you'?

What kind of a salesman are you?

Look, mate. I live in St Kilda, we have a high crime rate, my wife is at home alone a lot. I'm a prime bloody suspect for a sale on security doors.

You young blokes you gotta see that everything worth having is worth fighting for. Chasing a sale is like a champion footballer chasing a football. You never give up until the ball is in your hands. Who do you barrack for?

Who do you 'follow' in football?

That's not football, mate—nuh, nuh, don't give me that! Australian Rules is the most complicated beautiful ball game on Planet Earth. It's so many things—it's the most multifaceted of all football spectacles. There's no other game like it—Ah, you can take your Superbowl and... You try and beat the visual beauty of the high mark—or the perfect handpass—the goal kicked from an impossible angle. Mate, the bravery of the timely tackle, with no bloody body armour, mind you, and the teamwork—18 players, all finely tuned to each other—now that's art. My wife, she talks about Nureyev; but let me see VFL players playing to the best of their ability—let me marvel once again at the dance of Robbie Flower, the balletic leaps of Alex Jesaulenko, the lightning speed and courage of Syddie Jackson and the flamboyant fierce intelligent infuriating inferno that is Tiger Crosswell. That's why we go to Aussie Rules football, mate, and that's what keeps the supporters loyal to their teams.

You still there?

Good. You know what troubles me, mate? Our supporters come to the match week after week and they come with love and hope in their heart and what do they leave with? What do they leave with, when the players don't play to the best of their ability? Our supporters need us to show them a commitment to play the best game we can play. I'm sick of seeing them give up. I'm sick of seeing a man chase the ball like it's the ugliest girl on the dance floor. The ball, like your sale, is your dream girl! The ball is your chance to hold her and take both of you to glory.

He discards the phone and is now back at the MCG locker rooms.

The sounds of a crowd.

She's all you have to a better life, she's all you have to a perfect, happy life. I want you all to respect her, to follow her wherever she bounces and pull her off anyone who tries to touch her. The ball is the girl of your dreams. Don't you dare let the other side take her away!

The sounds of the crowd intensify as a scoreboard lights up the stage.

Say to yourself: 'If it is to be, it is up to me!'

MELBA *cranks the scoreboard to shows a win by Melbourne.*

The roar of the crowd.

SLIDE: Headline 'DEMONS SMASH WIN JINX'

If it is to be, it is up to me!

MELBA *cranks the scoreboard and cries out in happiness.*

Melbourne win against Footscray and Richmond.

SLIDE: Headline 'RON BRINGS DEVIL OUT IN DEMONS'

If it is to be, it is up to me!

Collingwood 15.20.110, Melbourne 11.12.78

MELBA: Sorry, Barass! Better luck next time!

She keeps cranking.
North Melbourne 16. 18. 114, Melbourne 10.5.65
Geelong 17.21.129, Melbourne 9.3.57

The scoreboard starts showing losses—loss after loss.

BARASSI *falls to his knees as headlines flash across the stage.*

SLIDE: Headline 'DEMONS TOWEL IT'

SLIDE: Headline 'BARASSI'S WORST YEAR'

SLIDE: Headline 'APPALLED, ASHAMED SAYS BARASSI'

SLIDE: Headline 'MELBOURNE BOTTOM OF THE LADDER AGAIN'

SLIDE: Headline 'BARASSI FAILURE WINS 33 LOSSES 77'

NORM SMITH *pulls down the banner: 'JUST HOW LONG DO WE WAIT BEFORE BECOMING WINNERS?'*

SLIDE: Headline 'BARASSI: WHY WE'RE FAILING'

SLIDE: Headline 'BEATEN BARASSI BOWS OUT'

SLIDE: Headline 'BYE, BYE, BARASS'

NORM *hands the banner to* BARASSI *who drags it offstage.*

When you overhear people say they don't like Australian Rules Football—feel sorry for them. Football fans shall not grow old as non-believers grow old. For a true follower of Australian Rules it shall always be three-quarter time with the scores level and a heart beating hope.

The stage is filled with trees lined in an avenue of honour. Some of the trees are soldiers with branches sticking out of them.

The image dissolves into a group of SOLDIERS *playing ball—they run off.*

What does our Super Coach do when his dreams are crushed? Barassi goes to the one person he badly needed to talk to all his life.

SCENE TWENTY-THREE: YOUNG DAD MEETS MIDDLE-AGED SON

SLIDE: Image of the military graveyard at Tobruk

There is a headstone that marks the grave of Ron James Barassi.

It reads:
  VX. 45220 Corporal
  R. J. BARASSI
  31 July 1941 Age 27
  ALWAYS REMEMBERED

CHERRYL *and* BARASSI *walk towards the grave, hand in hand.* CHERRYL *holds him tight and then leaves him beside the grave.* BARASSI *stares at the grave. Tears roll down his cheeks. He wipes perspiration off his brow and tears from his eyes. He blows his nose. He crouches down and is about to leave his mother's wedding ring on the grave then changes his mind. Another wave of grief overtakes him, mucus fills his throat and without thinking he spits on his father's grave.*

BARASSI: Sorry, Dad.

There is the sound of a giggle. BARASSI *joins in with the giggle.*

SENIOR: Did you just spit on my grave?

SENIOR *comes out from the shadows and sits down beside him.*

BARASSI: [*giggling and crying*] I'm so sorry, Dad, it's just, it's just…

SENIOR: It's fine, son.

BARASSI: It's just so bloody dry, stinking hot and my throat...

SENIOR: You get used to it.

BARASSI: How? How does anyone get used to this place?

SENIOR: The worst part was missing you and Elz.

BARASSI: It's a long way from home, Dad.

SENIOR: The way we all fought defending it—you'd think it was Toorak not bloody Tobruk.

BARASSI: You're so young.

SENIOR: And you're all grown-up.

BARASSI: You're just a kid.

SENIOR: That's what your mum used to say—drove me wild.

BARASSI: I'm nearly twice your age now.

SENIOR: What were you gonna leave for me?

BARASSI: [*handing him the ring*] Mum's wedding ring.

SENIOR *fondles the ring.*

SENIOR: It's not that worn down—

BARASSI: Well, she... eh... [remarried]

SENIOR: 'Course she did. You know football paid for this—if it wasn't for football I'd have had to give her the lid off a Tarax bottle, I reckon. Did you play football, son?

BARASSI: Yes, I played football.

SENIOR: And were you any good?

BARASSI: Was I good? Yeah, I did okay.

SENIOR: What position?

BARASSI: They invented a new position—ruck rover.

SENIOR: Ruck rover?

BARASSI: You were a rover.

SENIOR: I played in a premiership team.

BARASSI: I know. So did I.

SENIOR: Yeah?

BARASSI: Six.

SENIOR: Six?

BARASSI: Six premierships for Melbourne.

SENIOR: My Lord—I wished I'd seen that.

BARASSI: I wore your number 31.

SENIOR: My son, the champion football player.

BARASSI: I coached too!

SENIOR: My mate Norm wanted to coach.

BARASSI: He did.

SENIOR: Was Normie any good?

BARASSI: Better than me—he coached six Grand Final wins and I coached only four.

SENIOR: For Melbourne?

BARASSI: No. I coached Melbourne, but we never made it to the finals.

SENIOR: Six as a player and four as a coach. Wish I'd seen that.

BARASSI: So do I.

SENIOR: I missed everything.

BARASSI: There was this hollow feeling in my stomach when Mum said you were never coming home and I think I tried to fill that hole with winning, you know, always coming first like my father did.

SENIOR: I was the first person from Guildford to play VFL football and the first to play in a Grand Final. I was the first VFL footballer to be killed in the Second World War and the first soldier from my regiment to die of his wounds. Coming first—it's a bit overrated I reckon.

BARASSI: A lot from your regiment here?

SENIOR: And the rest. It's a United Bloody Nations: Poms, Indians, Poles, Germans, Irish—thousands of us.

BARASSI: Germans?

SENIOR: There's no fighting now.

BARASSI: I'm on my way to Ireland—to recruit Gaelic footballers. There's a boy there called Jim Stynes—got potential.

SENIOR: You know my mum's mum was Irish—your great grandmother—she liked the tipple, do you like the tipple, Ronny?

BARASSI: I do, I do. Me and the missus, we run a pub in Richmond.

SENIOR: A pub! By golly—what a dream of a life you have, boy. A dream of a life. Football, travel with a gorgeous woman and a pub, can't wait to tell my mates. [*He stares at the ring.*] You should give this ring to… [*He nods at* CHERRYL *in the distance.*] Is that your wife?

BARASSI: Yes.

SENIOR: She's a looker.

BARASSI: She's good to me and smarter than me—she's taught me diplomacy.

SENIOR: Much better looking too. Got kids?

BARASSI: You got three grandchildren, Dad—good kids all of them—not that I can take that much credit. I wasn't that great as a dad.

SENIOR: Bet you did better than me. [*Pause.*] Did Normie look after you? I asked him to.

BARASSI: Norm was bloody hard on me.

SENIOR: Good—you were a stubborn kid—got that from your mother.

BARASSI: Norm Smith missed you so much, Dad. He regretted all his life not going to war.

SENIOR: Norm! Here? He was so gung-ho! The way he always played from the front he'd have been dead in days of landing here or he'd have won the war for us a lot sooner.

BARASSI: I didn't miss you when I was a kid. Not having a dad was all I knew. But Christ, Christ I miss you now. I love you, Dad.

SENIOR: It's okay, little Ronny. Hey, don't you cry, little Ronny. Remember that day me and Norm busted you cutting down the rose bush?

BARASSI: Norm told me it was an apple tree.

SENIOR: It was a beautiful rose bush that I planted for your mother. I gave you such a hiding and you did not shed a tear, but you know something? I did. When I lay dying all I could think of was how sad it was that I'd never see that tough little boy of mine grow up. I'm so glad you came by, son.

> BARASSI *is fully crying now.* CHERRYL *comes and comforts him.*
>
> SENIOR *stands there smiling at them. He holds one arm out and walks towards* BARASSI. BARASSI *goes to shake his hand and* SENIOR *then walks straight past and shakes hands with a* SOLDIER GHOST *behind him.* BARASSI *has been fooled by the famous* BARASSI *handshake gag.*
>
> SENIOR *and the* SOLDIER *laugh like drains.* BARASSI *can't help but join in.*

CHERRYL: Are you okay, love?

> *More* SOLDIER GHOSTS *come out in uniform. They have come with*

a footy. They handpass it to SENIOR *who catches it easily.*

SERGEANT: Is that your boy, Ronny?

SENIOR: That's my boy, Sarg. You know he played in six premierships?

SERGEANT: Bullshit.

SENIOR: Played in my number 31.

PRIVATE: Keep your hat on, Corporal.

SENIOR: And he coached four premierships.

SERGEANT: Aah, Ronny, you were always one for tall tales.

SENIOR: And he either played or coached in 17 Grand Finals. Seventeen—go on, count 'em!

PRIVATE: [*taking the ball off* SENIOR] And I'm Roy Cazaly!

The SOLDIERS *run after the ball.*

BARASSI: [*looking at* SENIOR *but speaking to* CHERRYL] You know how I said we'd take his remains home?

CHERRYL: We'll bring him home.

BARASSI: No, love—we are going to leave him here with his mates.

SENIOR: I'm proud of you, son. I love you!

The SOLDIERS *chase the ball.*

BARASSI *holds* CHERRYL*'s hand.*

BARASSI: We got to go as well. We better get back to our happy ever after.

A beautiful sunset rises and the two walk towards it.

MELBA: And this is how the Legacy boy entered even this old one-eyed Collingwood supporter's heart.

CHERRYL: Have you given more thought to Ron Joseph's offer to coach the Swans?

WARWICK CAPPER, *a blonde, mullet-haired Sydney Swans player, in very short shorts, runs past and expertly handballs.*

BARASSI: You'd be running the pub on your own.

CHERRYL: Sydney Swans may no longer exist if you don't go.

BARASSI: If the AFL is to thrive, we must have Sydney.

CHERRYL: You might have to put your money where your bloody great mouth is, then!

EPILOGUE

MELBA: Now I never wanted the VFL to become a national game. I loved it when it was all about my suburbs—I'd even dispute the inclusion of Geelong, but Barassi went up north and saved the Sydney Swans from extinction. In 2005 he cried with joy when they won the Grand Final. To this day, Barassi's passion for life does not dim with age and neither does his ability to lift people to be better than they dreamt they could be. Some say they don't make men like Ron Barassi anymore. We hope they're bloody well wrong.

Delta Goodrem sings 'Together We Are One'.

The stage turns into shimmering water and MELBA *walks out with a torch. She hands it to* BARASSI.

He walks across the water to open the 2006 Commonwealth Games in Melbourne.

Black.

THE END

BY **TEE O'NEILL**

BARASSI

**TEE
O'NEILL**

WRITER

**TERENCE
O'CONNELL**

DIRECTOR

Tee O'Neill's writing has been awarded the Edward Albee Award, RE Ross Trust Playwright's Award, the Siena College International Play Award and a Residency at the Royal Court Theatre in London. She has been nominated twice for the Griffin Award, Patrick White Award and Corcadorca Play of the Year in Ireland, once for the NSW Premier's Award, Australian Writer's Guild award, New Dramatists Award in NYC, and a Wal Cherry Award. She has been an Affiliate Writer for the Melbourne Theatre Company and been produced and commissioned by Sydney Theatre Company, Playbox, Theatre @ Risk, White Whale Theatre and New York University. She is working with a Film Victoria grant to adapt her Play Best Possible World into a film script.

Tee has been a lecturer in scriptwriting for thirteen years including playwriting residencies at the New York University (School of TISCH) Otago University, National University of Singapore and lecturer at LASALLE College of the Arts in Singapore. She is playwriting co-ordinator at Melbourne University.

Terence is a NIDA Graduate who has staged some 150 productions in theatres, circus tents, concert halls, comedy clubs and cabaret rooms across Australia and internationally.

His best known productions include *Bouncers*, *Certified Male*, *Buddy-The Buddy Holly Story*, Steven Berkoff's *Decadence*, *I Only Want To Be With You-The Dusty Springfield Story* and *Minefields And Miniskirts-Australian Women And The Vietnam War*.

For The Production Company at Melbourne's State Theatre, Terence has directed an acclaimed series of classic Broadway musicals including *Oklahoma!*, *42nd. Street* and *The King & I*.

Recent projects include *Motherhood-The Musical* (National Tour) and *The Kitchen Sink* (Red Stitch Actors Theatre). He next directs *Whitney: The Greatest Love Of All* (Johannesburg) and *Cruising Paradise-Sam Shepard Stories* at 45 Downstairs. Terence is currently writing *Over The Top: Helena Rubinstein & I*.

Dedicated to my dad, Denis O'Neill, and to all dads who encourage their children to dream. TO'N

EXECUTIVE PRODUCER'S NOTE

The concept of BARASSI was formulated in September 2010 when I saw the Broadway production of LOMBARDI which depicted the life of legendary US football coach, Vince Lombardi. Believing theatre has a responsibility to reflect its own society, I started writing notes, in the theatre, in the dark.

Upon returning to Australia, I engaged playwright, Tee O'Neill, met with legendary Australian Rules footballer and coach, Ron Barassi, and received his blessing and best wishes and embarked upon the enormous task of depicting the life of a true Australian hero on stage.

Ron Barassi is, metaphorically, and actually, a larger than life person. He was my childhood hero, growing up in football mad Melbourne in the 1960s and he remains a hero to many of my generation and now to a new generation, after his brave efforts in rushing to the defence of a woman being bashed in the street when he was 72 years old.

His story, commencing in World War II and spanning several decades, has been beautifully pieced together in a dramatic and epic fashion by the writer, Tee O'Neill, has been artfully directed by Terence O'Connell, and beautifully brought to life by the fabulous cast and creative crew.

I hope BARASSI continues to enthrall audiences long after we are all gone.

Alan D Jager

AUTHOR'S NOTE

This is a theatrical imagining of one person's life seen through the eyes of the amateur historian, Melba. The events within the play have been authenticated from the public domain, through newspaper articles, commentary and replays and from talking to hundreds of people, some who were at the heart of the events, others on the side. Many stories came to me unsolicited – as soon as I mentioned I was writing this play, rarely would I not hear a new Barassi story and I thank everyone who told me what they heard, saw or felt about the icon.

Tee O'Neill

CHRIS ASIMOS

AMANDA LABONTE

Chris Asimos grew up in South Australia and is an honours graduate of the Flinders University Drama Centre - but he now calls Melbourne home. Since graduating, Chris has worked steadily in theatre, film and television. Some of his many stage credits include Three Sisters, The Give & Take, Everynight, Everynight and Boy's Life (Curtain Call Award Nominee). Musical theatre credits include *Scratch* in the Japanese premiere of Once Upon a Midnight, and most recently *Sportacu*s in the Australian tour of Lazytown for Echelon Productions.

Chris's screen appearances include *Sgt Gunner* and *Lt Nash* in the cult SBS TV series Danger 5, *Chris* in the feature Double Happiness Uranium and *Bill* in the short film Bad Language, which showcased at MIFF in 2010. Chris is thrilled to be part of this exciting stage premiere of Barassi.

Amanda studied at The University of Ballarat and works as an actor and theatre producer. The core of her producing work has been with the creation, development and management of Essential Theatre.

She has spent many years performing in Essential Theatre's tour of *Shakespeare in the Vines* – an annual tour of Shakespearian comedies to Australian and New Zealand wineries. Credits include Beatrice in *Much Ado About Nothing,* Helena in *A Midsummer Night's Dream*, Maria in *Twelfth Night*, Lady Capulet in *Romeo and Juliet* and Luciana in *The Comedy of Errors*.

In 2011 she creatively developed and performed in *A Stranger in Town* at fortyfive downstairs.

Television credits include Neighbours, Blue Heelers, Back Berner and Dogwoman - most recently in the Australian feature film, *The Cup*.

She is thrilled to be part of *Barassi*.

STEVE BASTONI

JANE CLIFTON

One of Australia's most accomplished actors, Steve`s string of film and television credits include the Golden Globe nominated *On The Beach.* He became a household name as 'Angel' in *Police Rescue* and has starred in numerous TV productions including *The Magistrate, South Pacific,* the award winning mini-series *Blue Murder and, Underbelly The Golden Mile.*

Steve's theatre credits include the Company B production of *Threepenny Opera*, the Cameron Macintosh production of *Oliver* under the direction of Sam Mendes and Ben Elton's *Popcorn.* Steve's most recent theatre production was *Everynight, Everynight* at Gasworks this year, a revival of Ray Mooney's gritty prison play which opened to rave reviews.

His film credits include *Heartbreak Kid, 15 Amore(AFI nomination Matrix Reloaded, Macbeth (M),* and *Suburban Mayhem.* This year, Steve will be starring opposite Sam Worthington in the surf drama *Drift.*

Jane Clifton BA is an actress, singer, writer and marriage celebrant! She appeared at La Mama, the Pram Factory, the Flying Trapeze, TF Much Ballroom and the Last Laugh Theatre Restaurant.
She was in Division 4, Homicide, Ryan, Bluey, even Holiday Island and of course Margo in Prisoner/ Cell-Block H!

She fronted the feminists-on-Countdown band Stiletto and had top 10 pop singles Girl on the Wall and Taxi Mary (with Jo Jo Zep). Her solo CD The Marriage of Style was released in 2003.

She toured in Pack of Women, smash-hit stage shows Mum's the Word and Menopause – the Musical.

Jane's first novel Half Past Dead, a 'girly, sexy, thriller', was published in 2002. The follow-up, A Hand in the Bush , was published in 2005. Her latest book The Address Book - a memoir of the 32 houses Jane has lived was published in 2011.

BARASSI—The Stage Show
Match starts 7.30 pm

CHARACTER	G	B		CAST	G	B
Barassi				**Steve Bastoni**		
Barassi Jr				**Chris Asimos**		
Barassi Sr				**Chris Asimos**		
Capper				**Russell Robertson**		
Cherryl				**Amanda LaBonte**		
Colin				**Glenn Maynard**		
Crosswell				**Russell Robertson**		
Elza				**Amanda LaBonte**		
Froggy				**Sean McGrath**		
Harris				**Richard Sutherland**		
Harrison				**Russell Robertson**		
Hopkins				**Amanda LaBonte**		
Jesaulenko				**Sean McGrath**		
Kyne				**Richard Sutherland**		
Manassa				**Russell Robertson**		
Mantello				**Richard Sutherland**		
Mark				**Russell Robertson**		
Melba				**Jane Clifton**		
Mueller				**Richard Sutherland**		
Nancy				**Amanda LaBonte**		
Norm				**Matthew Parkinson**		
Syd				**Glenn Maynard**		
Tuddenham				**Russell Robertson**		
Weideman				**Sean McGrath**		

Jager Productions supporting

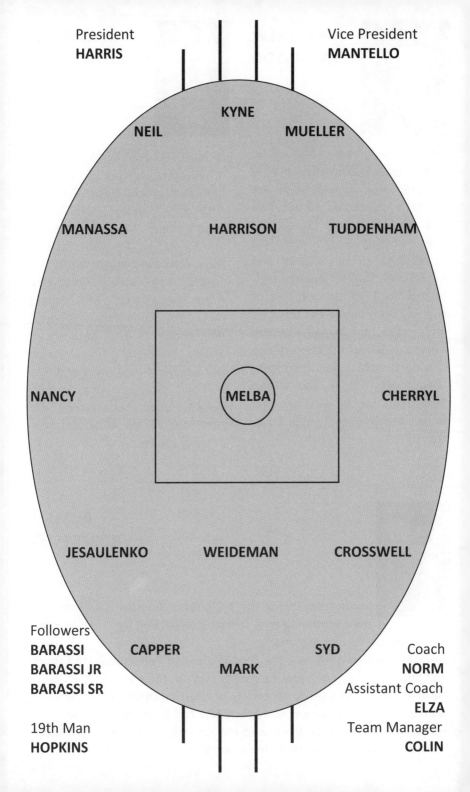

MATTHEW PARKINSON

RICHARD SUTHERLAND

Matt is best known to Melbourne audiences as a comedian and radio presenter, as well as for his regular appearances on ABC-TV's 'The Einstein Factor'. He has also been working as an actor for more than 25 years. Born and raised in Perth, he moved to Melbourne in 1987 as one half of comedy duo 'Empty Pockets'. He also found time to win the top prizes on 'Sale of the Century'. He is a passionate supporter of the West Coast Eagles and is delighted to be in a show that brings together footy and theatre.

Richard Sutherland, BA appeared in several college productions. His film credits include *Face To Face*, *Red Hill*, *Playing for Charlie*, *Square One*, *Muriel's Wedding* and *Metal Skin*. TV credits include *Bikie Wars: Brothers In Arms*, *The Straits*, *Rush*, *Killing Time*, *City Homicide*, *Tangle*, *Dirt Game*, *McLeod's Daughters*, *Stingers*, *Blue Heelers*, *The Man From Snowy River*, *Halifax fp*, *Police Rescue*, *Home and Away* and *Sins – Envy*. Stage credits include *Kelly's Reign*, *Testosterone*, *De Niro - Behind the Mask* and *Puppetry of the Penis*.

RUSSELL ROBERTSON

Robbo played for the Melbourne Football Club and sits third on the all time Demon goal kicking list. He also regularly took spectacular high marks.

He has appeared on Nine's *The Footy Show* and Ten's *Before the Game* and Seven's *It takes two* making it all the way to the grand final.

He danced in the closing ceremony of the Commonwealth Games in Melbourne and sang a duet with Olivia Newton-John live on the MCG.

He plays in a corporate group with Phil Ceberano and hosts *The Robbo Show* for Melbourne Football Club's web site.

GLENN MAYNARD

SEAN McGRATH

Glenn Maynard is an actor, musician, comedian and writer. He is Aboriginal and vegan. He has had guest roles in Neighbours, Triple Zero Heroes and Stingers. Short film credits include with Mooncake and Crab. He played 'Nookie' in Michael Rymer's 'Face To Face'. Music experience includes writing, recording, performing and producing. In 2012 he performed in Cambodia as country music's prodigal son, 'Gareth Rivers'. His writing credits include Channel 31's 'Stuff' 'Darren and Greg' (Carlton Courthouse - Fringe Festival) and website content. Currently, he is shooting an independent black/comedy feature 'Chocolate, Vanilla, Strawberry'.

Sean's theatre credits include *Fiddler on the Roof, Cats, The Wizard of Oz, Chicago(UK tour), Copacabana, Shout, The Producers* and *Priscilla Queen of the Desert the Musical*. He performed in *La Traviata* and *Lakme* for Opera Australia and *The Pajama Game*. More recently he played the role of Aaron in *Chicago* (Australisian tour). TV credits include the *Helpmann Awards, The Footy Show, Aria Awards, Good Morning Australia, Lily Savage Live* (UK), *The Logie Awards, In Melbourne Tonight* and *Dancing with the Stars*. He has performed with Kate Ceberano and Tina Arena and has appeared in the Australian feature films *Josh Jarmen* and *Strange Bedfellows.*

ACKNOWLEDGEMENTS

The World Premiere Season of BARASSI was made possible by:

- LINE PRODUCER — Simon Myers
- PRODUCTION MANAGER — Tom Webster
- STAGE MANAGER — Ashley Groenen

Head electrics: Gordon Boyd; Lighting Programmer: Harrison Cope; Vision Technician: Olaf Meyer; Sound Crew: Tony Day & Tim Bright; Costume Supervisor/Dresser: Deb Hallam; Wigs: Corrine Day; Set Builder: Peter Turley; Mechanist: Josh Punchen; Publicity: Cavanagh PR; Marketing: Zebra PI, Craig Martin Media.

SPECIAL THANKS

Meg Upton, Denis O'Neill, Tony O'Neill, Danny O'Neill, Eddie Crawley, Odette Joannidis, Tony Charlton, Ian Brayshaw, Sam Mancuso, Kiem-Ai Nguyen, Yasmin Mitchell, Tanya Healey, Glenn Elston, Greg Hocking, Peter Matheson, Dr Kit Lazaroo, Paul Monaghan, Peter Eckersall, Robert Flower, Andrew Mansour, 3 Deep Design, Kaspa at Alook Production Services, Michael at Event Equipment and MultiMedia Events Australia. MultiMedia Events Australia.

NATHAN WEYERS
SET DESIGN

JASON BOVAIRD
LIGHTING DESIGN

Nathan has been involved in over 80 productions, in drama, opera, dance, puppetry, film and musical theatre. He has a Bachelor of Performing Arts - Design for Performance. He has worked on *Phantom of the Opera*, *Swan Lake* and *West Side Story* and toured with *Dr Zhivago* and *Disney's Mary Poppins* around Australia, NZ and Singapore. He has designed over 30 productions on a national and international scale and has been nominated multiple times by the Victorian Music Theatre Guild and been awarded for Excellence in Scenic Design, most recently in BLOC Music Theatre's *Singin' In the Rain*.

Jason has been a freelance lighting designer for the past 12 years and has lit over 300 productions both in Australia and overseas including Los Angeles, London and New Zealand having worked along side Broadway and West End lighting designer Ken Billington in New York. His highly acclaimed lighting designs have included shows such as *Motherhood – The Musical* (2011 Aust. Tour), *Busting Out* (Australia, Los Angeles, London, Scotland, New Zealand), *2008 Victorian State Schools Spectacular*, *Dumped – The Musical* and *Miss Saigon*. Jason has received 3 Victorian Music Theatre Guild awards for his highly acclaimed lighting designs throughout Victoria.

KIM BISHOP
COSTUME DESIGN

For *The Production Company* Kim was Costume Designer for *Sweet Charity*, *42nd Street*, *Damn Yankees*, *Mame*, *Crazy For You*, *The Boyfriend*, *The King & I*, *Kismet*, *The Producers*, and for the highly successful *The Boy From Oz*. He has toured as Wardrobe Manager on many large scale musicals including *The King & I*, *South Pacific*, *Rocky Horror Show*, *Aida – The Spectacular*, *Crazy For You*, *Singin' In The Rain*, *The Boy From Oz* and *Dusty*. Kim has toured the world with *Torvill & Dean*, playing everywhere from Melbourne to Las Vegas, Madison Square Garden and Wembley. Web site - kimbishop.com.au

PAUL NORTON
SOUND DESIGN

GEORGIE PINN
VISUAL DESIGN

Paul was signed to Mushroom Records in 1981 with The Runners and went on to have a solo National Hit with Stuck On You in 1989 reaching no 2 on the Australian Charts. He performed A Southern Sky at the 2000 Olympics in Sydney. Paul was Musical Director and wrote the score for The Australian Shakespeare's production of Much Ado About Nothing, Macbeth, Jungle Book and the finale for the critically acclaimed comedy Certified Male. He toured Australia with the Countdown Spectacular featuring Australia's top Rock Acts of the eighties; performing to 100,000 people nationwide.

Georgie Pinn is an Artist/Director of Motion graphics and began her career creating and editing music videos for bands and visual concepts for their live productions.

For 14 years she has worked across Europe and Asia designing special effects, sound and animation for TV and the live arena.

These skills combined have also paved the way for the creation of animated sets and live triggered projection installations for the theatre, dance, music and fashion industry.

ALANA SCANLAN
CHOREOGRAPHY

Alana Scanlan is one of Australia's most in-demand choreographers, working in theatre, fashion, commercials, music clips and bespoke corporate events.
Her new theatre work includes, *I Only Want To Be With You-The Dusty Springfield Story, Certified Male, Minefields and Miniskirts* and most recently *Dumped!-The Musical.* She has choreographed numerous stage musicals, including eight for The Production Company at The State Theatre of Victoria. Alana has that rare ability to work across many different styles and mediums. A long list of TV credits, along with numerous public events and ceremonies, movies, live television concerts and production shows is testament to her versatility and vision.

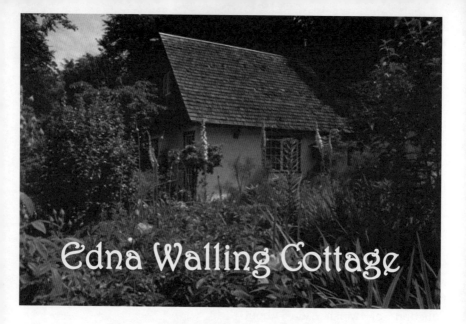

Edna Walling Cottage

Bed & Breakfast

6 Sherbrooke Road Sherbrooke, Victoria

SET ON 3 ACRES, THIS HERITAGE LISTED 1936 COTTAGE WAS ORIGINALLY BUILT AS A FULL-SIZED DOLLS' HOUSE AND IS LOCATED AMIDST EDNA WALLING'S "GREATEST ACHIEVEMENT", *MAWARRA,* DESCRIBED BY EDNA HERSELF AS "A SYMPHONY IN STEPS AND BEAUTIFUL TREES". EDNA WALLING COTTAGE IS CLOSE TO A SELECTION OF RESTAURANTS AND CAFES AND IS METRES FROM SHERBROOKE FOREST. WINERIES AND BERRY FARMS ARE NEARBY. IT COMPRISES LOUNGE, GAS LOG FIRE, TV & DVD, KITCHEN, BATHROOM AND UPSTAIRS QUEEN-SIZED BEDROOM.

PH: 03 9755 1273
EMAIL: BOOKINGS@EDNAWALLING.NET.AU